The Indispensable Parson

William Cowper (1778–1858)

The Life and Influence of
Australia's First Parish Clergyman

Peter G. Bolt

Studies in Australian Colonial History 2:
Commemorative Pictorial Edition

William Cowper (1778–1858): The Indispensable Parson. The Life and Influence of Australia's First Parish Clergyman. Commemorative Pictorial Edition

© Bolt Publishing Services, **2009, 2021**

www.boltpublishing.com.au

STUDIES IN AUSTRALIAN COLONIAL HISTORY

1. Thomas Moore of Liverpool: One of Our Oldest Colonists.

    Essays & Addresses to Celebrate 15 Years of Moore College.

2. William Cowper (1778–1858): The Indispensable Parson. The Life and Influence of Australia's First Parish Clergyman.

    – Full Text Edition
    – Commemorative Pictorial Edition

National Library of Australia Cataloguing-in-Publication entry

Author:	Bolt, Peter, 1958–
Title:	William Cowper (1778–1858): the indispensable parson: the life and influence of Australia's first parish clergyman /Peter G. Bolt.
Edition:	Ingram Edition 2022
ISBN:	978-0-9946349-8-6 (Paperback) 978-0-9946349-9-3 (e-version)
Series:	Studies in Australian colonial history, 2
Notes:	Includes index. Bibliography.
Subjects:	Church of England—Australia—History Cowper, William, 1778–1858. Clergy—Australia—Biography Australia—Church history
Dewey Number:	283.94092

Design and layout by Lankshear Design Pty Ltd. Phone: 02 9868 7044.
Printed by: Whirlwind Print. Phone: 1300 129 227.

Preface

On 19th August 1809, when William disembarked from the *Indispensable* with his family, he commenced a ministry at the church of St Phillip, Sydney, which he sustained for just short of fifty years. Once Cowper was inducted to the recently-created Parish of Sydney, he gave himself to his parishioners until the end of his life. Although there had been other Chaplains in the colony before him, he can rightly be called Australia's first parish clergyman.

In 1901, when William's first Australian-born son, William Macquarie, penned his *Autobiography and Reminiscences*, he hoped 'to give an accurate description of his [father's] life, work, and character' in order to make known 'to the present generation how he lived and laboured for the welfare of the land in which they dwell'. True to the clergyman's profession shared by both father and son, W. Macquarie had a reformative aim in mind:

> *It is my earnest hope and prayer that those who may read these pages may be animated by the same spirit and zeal for the public good as he was inspired with, and may strive to imitate his example. Such religion as that which he possessed is a power for good far more effective in its moral results than great wealth or high honour.*[1]

When Cowper's descendants gathered together to celebrate the 175th Anniversary of his arrival, William's life was once again briefly recounted to reinspire a new generation. Those who attended the occasion at St Philip's were given a brochure that made these intentions clear:

> *We, his descendants, should be thankful to God for his life and for his example to others, including ourselves. Let us ensure that succeeding generations are ever mindful of their proud heritage, reflecting in their lives those qualities which William Cowper exemplified in his long and outstanding ministry.*[2]

The 2009 Bicentennial provides the opportunity to re-examine, to remember and to celebrate the life and influence of William Cowper. Perhaps, once again, yet another new generation will find inspiration here. Perhaps this inspiration will then produce further benefit in the various communities that make up the nation that William's long and faithful work helped to build.

---

1. W.M. Cowper, *Autobiography & Reminiscences*, 73.
2. Cowper Family, 'Commemoration of the 175th Anniversary', 23.

New South Wales, New Zealand, New Hebrides and the Islands Adjacent, 1808.
Robert Wilkinson (d. ca. 1825). National Library of Australia: nla.map-T1363.

1 | An Englishman comes to Sydney
(1778–1809) | Vision Inspires Action

*O*N FRIDAY THE 18TH AUGUST 1809, as the *Indispensable* brought the next load of white settlers through the sheer cliffs and the harbour opened up before their eyes, they caught a glimpse of why it was reputed to be the best in the world. The vessel manoeuvred through Port Jackson under the watchful eye of Captain Henry Best. From the shore, other watchful eyes followed its progress towards where earlier whites had built a settlement. What was left of the indigenous Cadigal band may have wondered what this latest wave would bring to their land. They probably saw the new arrivals crowding on the deck and looking across the water. They could not have seen that one of these white men would soon plead for the 'Eora' people, being deeply moved by signs of their imminent obliteration.

A View of Sydney from Seven Miles, J.W. Lewin, 1809. State Library of NSW: PXA 388 V.3 f.1.

With the hustle and bustle of the sailors above and around, William Cowper drank in the sight of the hills, covered with unfamiliar timber running all the way to the water's edge. No-one would use the name 'Australia' for at least another five years. Back in Hull, when they prayed for his journey, they used the old name, 'Botany Bay'. When the British Government had sent him here, along with his new bride and his four young children, he was commissioned Assistant Chaplain to 'New South Wales'. But as he looked out on the sprawling settlement around the cove in which the vessel dropped anchor, and thought of the native inhabitants of the country, William saw a small part of the Lord's harvest field, now placed under his pastoral care. When he stepped ashore on Saturday, he did so as the first clergyman in the Parish of Sydney. Once arrived, his vision kept him active for almost 50 years.

In 1809 hardly anyone even noticed William Cowper's arrival. At his funeral in 1858 an estimated 25,000 people—one third of Sydney—lined the streets. He came to NSW unknown, but after patiently pursuing his vision for 49 years, when Sydney said its last goodbye, he had become the indispensable parson.

William Cowper was born on 28 December 1778 in Whittington, Lancashire. The Cowper family roots, however, stretched some 13 miles northwards along the Lune Valley, to Sedbergh, a village in the West Riding of Yorkshire. This was where William's father, farmer Samuel Cowper, married his mother Isabella Sedgwick (25 May 1768). Their first child, Leonard, was born in Sedbergh (3 March 1769), but by the time John was born, they were living at Sellet Hall, a property in the hills to the north of Whittington, close enough to have him christened at St Michael the Archangel (22 October 1775). This was the Parish church in which they also christened the next two boys, William (20 June 1779) and Thomas (1 October 1781).

Not much is known about William's early days. The family remained at Sellet Hall until 1787. Although once he had settled in Australia William owned land and also had the odd cow running on—or out of!—his Glebe, and acquired other land, he did not seem to share the same love and aptitude for farming as that of the earlier chaplains Richard Johnson and Samuel Marsden. Instead of farming skills, his father may have passed on other things to his son, who was known for his love of learning throughout his adult days. A late report suggests that it was Samuel who largely educated William at home. Another report, however, has him educated at the Sedbergh Free Grammar School.

As a young man William had great facility in mathematics and he enjoyed submitting answers to mathematical puzzles published in

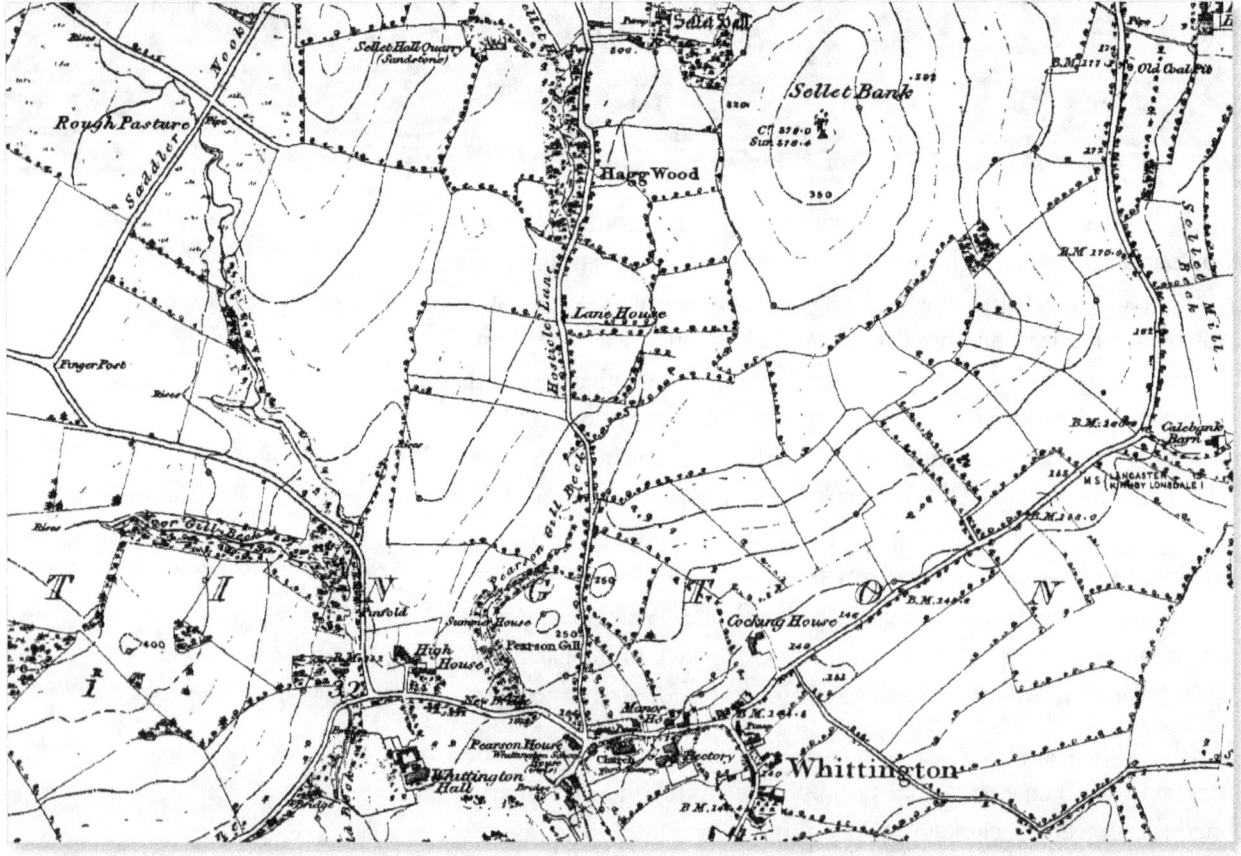

Sellet Hall, Whittington, the Cowper home until 1787, can be seen top centre.

Map of Whittington. www.old-maps.co.uk © website and database right "Crown Copyright and Landmark Information Group Ltd" (*All rights reserved 2009*).

Evans House and St Andrew's Sedbergh

'Evans House' by Henry Bracken, ca. 1930. Watercolour. Courtesy: Sedbergh School Archive and Heritage Centre.

some popular magazines of the day. A high-point came when his work achieved a published correction to the *Course of Mathematics* by Charles Hutton, distinguished teacher at the Royal Military College, Woolwich. William's acknowledged mathematical ability places him in a stream of leading mathematical minds that were emerging from Sedbergh at this period. Since the source of these upcoming scholars was John Dawson, a self-taught mathematical genius, who was also the local physician at Sedbergh, it is highly probable that William also sat at this man's feet.

Apparently William did not show any early leaning towards the ministry, although the area had plenty of Christian influences that may have helped to shape him in this direction. Presumably his family connections continued with parish churches such as Whittington and Sedbergh. The Sedbergh School had a strong Protestant ethos. The district had played a key role in the early expansion of Quakerism, and it still felt this influence. John Dawson himself stood within this tradition of 'old dissent'. George Whitefield had preached in the district, but as for 'new dissent', the Methodists had made little impact by the time of William's youth. A late nineteenth century suggestion that William was greatly influenced by Bunyan's *Pilgrim's Progress* is probably a good guess, given the importance of this book in Protestant circles.

Portrait of John Dawson (1734–1820), 1809. William Whiston Barney, after Joseph Allen. © National Portrait Gallery, London. NPG D8262.

But in the only explicit comment on his Christian influences that has survived from William's own mouth, it is his elder brother to whom he wishes to repay his spiritual debts. Towards the end of his days, William wrote to John, reminding him of a Christian tract he had given him when he was about eight years old. This printed sermon (on Micah 2:10) had made such an impression on the boy, it remained

CHAPTER 1 | AN ENGLISHMAN COMES TO SYDNEY (1778–1809)

vivid in the memory of the old man as he wrote just eighteen months before he died: 'Having obtained help of Him, I continue to this day, and have been led to think more and more of the grace and mercy, goodness and love, wisdom and power of God, as manifested in the wonderful plan devised for fallen man's eternal Redemption, into which the Holy angels desire to look'. This vision, once caught, continued to inspire William to action.

In 1796, at the age of 17, William moved to Northallerton, North Yorkshire, where he became tutor to a clergyman's family—most probably, his pupils were the younger boys of Rev. Benjamin Walker, long-serving Vicar of All Saints Church.

St Mary the Virgin, Richmond, Marriage Register. North York County Record Office: PR/RM 1/6.

This was a tense time for England, and the worsening situation with France called for extra manpower to be at the ready. After being disembodied in 1783, the North York Militia had been re-embodied in 1792, in Northallerton. In 1795 rumours circulated of a huge army led by Napoleon Bonaparte about to launch a three-pronged invasion of England. The nation further prepared itself for war. In December 1797, the North York Militia embodied a Supplementary force. In July 1798, William Cowper joined this 2nd North York Militia, now at Richmond, Yorkshire, as part of Captain Hobson's newly formed company, earning 1 shilling a day as a private.

In October 1798, the 2nd NY marched to Glasgow, and later Edinburgh, where they were involved in escorting French prisoners of war. However, whilst doing his duty in the interests of national security, William's heart

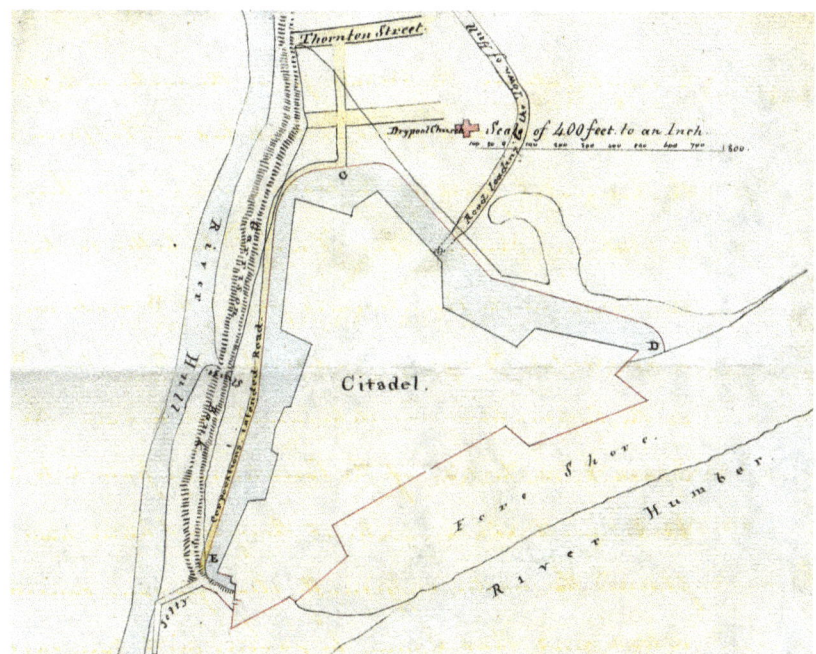

St Peter's Drypool is in red at the top of this map, signed by Cowper's commanding officer, S.R. Chapman, 1806.
National Archives-UK: WO 55/714.

was probably turning to other things. By taking him to Richmond, his enlistment in the Militia had enabled him to meet Hannah Horner. One thing led to another, and on 11 April 1799 the twenty-year-old William married his blushing bride of about sixteen at St Mary the Virgin, Richmond. Soon after the wedding, Cowper transferred to a different company, whose June marching orders took him to Hull.

By the end of the year, England took further steps towards vigorously prosecuting the war with France. When incentives were offered for militiamen to join the regular infantry and artillery, many from the North York Militia enlisted. Once they were replaced from the ranks of the Supplementary Militia, it was too depleted to continue. And so, on the 5 December 1799, William's militia career came to an end.

William and Hannah now set up home in Drypool, near Hull. Here they had the joy of the arrival of their first child, Henry, who was born in June 1800 and baptised on 17 August 1800, at St Peter's Church, Drypool. Two years later they were blessed with their second son, Thomas, born 23 October 1802. Mary Stephenna was born around January 1805 and baptised at St Peter's on 6 March, and on 26 April 1807, William and Hannah rejoiced at the birth of their fourth child, Charles.

At Henry's baptism, the register still listed William's occupation as a 'soldier'. His next place of employment is not known, but we do know that his conscience led him to resign from this position. Despite the obvious difficulties it brought him—with a wife and two children to support at the time—when he was required to work on the Sabbath day, his only choice was to leave.

William had fallen in with the strongly evangelical circles at Hull at this time. William Wilberforce, later famous as the anti-slavery reformer, held the patronage of St Peter's Drypool. The clergymen Joseph Milner, Josiah Rodwell, Thomas Dykes, and John Scott were popular and influential preachers in the town. Amongst these men, keeping the

Thomas Dykes (1761–1847) Memorial. Charterhouse, Hull. Courtesy: The Master, L.S. Deas. Photo: Martin & Lynne Broom.

CHAPTER 1 | AN ENGLISHMAN COMES TO SYDNEY (1778–1809)

ABOVE LEFT: Goff & Amey's portrait of Richard Johnson. When William was in London, early in 1809, he was contacted at Goff & Amey's address.
Revd. Richard Johnson, B.A., Chaplain to the Settlement in New South Wales, 1787. G. Terry. National Library of Australia: nla.pic-an9594799.

ABOVE RIGHT: *Revd S. Marsden formerly Senior Chaplain of N.S. Wales, and founder of the New Zealand Mission*. Unknown artist. Richard Jones' album. Pencil portrait. State Library of NSW: PXA 972/5.

Sabbath was a crucial part of Christian obedience, and its observance was something of a touch-stone of the health of society in general.

The next salaried position that we know of was in April 1804, when William was appointed as the Clerk of Works for the Royal Engineers Department at Hull. He remained in this position until just before he was due to leave for New South Wales.

The evangelicals of Hull already had a strong interest in NSW. Richard Johnson and Samuel Marsden, the first two Chaplains sent to the colony at the other side of the world, were both Yorkshiremen. They had both attended Hull Grammar School, then under the influence of Joseph Milner, the leading evangelical of the town. Both men were also associated with the network of evangelicals that stretched from Hull to Clapham, in London, which had taken a keen interest in NSW since before the First Fleet.

When his conscience forced William Cowper to leave his job, a group of friends urged him to consider entering the ministry. He had no doubt already become acquainted with the Rev. Thomas Dykes, and now the influential preacher of St John the Evangelist, Hull, encouraged him in this direction. Following the usual pattern for preparing someone for Holy Orders, Dykes set Cowper a course of theological reading which would, eventually, equip him well for his long ministry in NSW.

During this period, Cowper probably also came under the influence of another man who helped to shape his future. About the same time that Cowper first arrived in Hull, Rev. John Scott became Dykes' curate.

In August 1801, Scott left in order to become Lecturer of Holy Trinity, Hull, and Master of the Grammar School, in the place of Rev. Josiah Rodwell who had died. To replace him at St John's, Dykes appointed Rev. Richard Johnson. Bruised and battered by his time at 'Botany Bay', and feeling rather financially ill-treated by the Government, Johnson had been forced to take a curacy. Presumably his need had filtered through the network which connected him and Dykes, and so he came to St John's, where he served for a little over two years. Thus, one of Hull's own missionaries, who never lost his interest in NSW, was available to help develop Cowper's vision, to 'lift up his eyes to see that the fields were white for harvest' (John 4:35) in the place the locals still called 'Botany Bay'.

Samuel Marsden to Miles Atkinson, 19 May 1803. National Library of Australia: MS 4049.

Johnson's departure from Sydney in October 1800 had left Samuel Marsden as Principal Chaplain. Despite his own ox-like strength and tireless activity, Marsden was soon putting out feelers for an assistant amongst the evangelicals that had been his own constant supporters. In May 1803 he wrote to Rev. Miles Atkinson, a leading figure in the Elland Society, which had put Marsden through university:

> I wish that some person could be sent out to assist me. […] Should you have any young man belonging to the Society fit for this situation, I should be exceeding happy if he could be sent out […]. He must be married, have a good Constitution, not afraid of toil and labour, and have by nature an active turn of mind. Such a young man would be very acceptable in this Country; and might be very useful.[1]

1. Samuel Marsden to Miles Atkinson, 19 May 1803 (National Library of Australia MS 4049).

CHAPTER 1 | AN ENGLISHMAN COMES TO SYDNEY (1778–1809)

Marsden hoped to find lay settlers to begin the work of the Church Missionary Society in New Zealand.

Station of the Church Missionary Society at Te Puna, Bay of Islands, seen from the SSE, 1840–1849. Augustus Earle (1793–1838). National Library of Australia: nla.pic-an2260373.

Since Atkinson was one of Dykes' close friends, presumably the preacher of St John's would also be placed on the alert. If he found such a potentially 'useful' young man, there was a position for him already waiting. By the time Atkinson was reading this letter, Cowper was probably already reading for the ministry under Dykes' supervision.

By 1806 Marsden had secured permission to return to England on a recruiting drive. Once this man on a mission stepped off the *Buffalo* on 10 November 1807, a whirlwind sequence of events was set in motion. First he gained authority from the Government to find two extra chaplains, and the blessing of the committee of the fledgling Church Missionary Society to find two missionaries to work amongst the Maoris. He then headed towards the regions he still called home. Passing through Norfolk, he visited Richard Johnson, now at Bunwell, where he presumably sought his old friend's advice, and this most probably included a young man named Cowper. On arriving at Hull, he soon made Cowper's acquaintance, and invited William to join him in NSW. By late November, Cowper had already requested leave of absence from the Royal Engineers. In January 1808, he received a commission as Chaplain for NSW. On 20 March he was made Deacon, and on 10 April ordained Priest. By the end of May, he had finally resigned from the Engineers and ceased work, sent the family's luggage to Portsmouth to be stowed on the *Aeolus*, and he was short of cash. When he wrote to the Secretary of State to see if he could gain a further advance on his salary, he outlined his plans: Leave Hull on the 6th June, settle some business in London on the 8th, travel to Portsmouth to meet the convoy in time to sail.

Hull Packet, 14 June 1808.

Marriage Licence Allegation, William Cowper & Ann Barrell, 21 Jan 1809. Lambeth Palace Library: FM I/147.

Samuel Stones to William Cowper, sent to the address of 'Goff & Amey', supporters of Richard Johnson. 17 Jan 1809. Keith Cowper Family Archive.

CHAPTER 1 | AN ENGLISHMAN COMES TO SYDNEY (1778–1809)

But the Cowpers never made it to Portsmouth.

On the day William planned to leave Hull, Hannah had already fallen sick. Marsden, in Hull at the time to bid them farewell, wrote on the 7th still hopeful that she would recover and the Cowpers would make the *Aeolus*. Within days the severity of the illness had become plain, and by the end of the week, she had died. William was now sole parent to four young children—Henry now eight, Charles force-weaned by his mother's untimely death. William's plans had to change radically.

It is difficult to trace Cowper's movements in the next few months. He was still engaged in ministry at Drypool in August. In the closing months of the year, he was probably assisting Rev. Samuel Stones at Rawdon, while the family continued to live at Hull. As the new year opened, he was in London, living in the parish of St Mary's, Newington Butts. He had left the north with hopes of finding a wife to accompany him to NSW, and, on 21 January, he married 26 year old Ann Barrell. Her future son would one day describe her as 'a lady who proved herself a true mother to his children, and a valuable helper to himself in his ministry'.

Port Jackson, New South Wales, 1825.
Augustus Earle (1793–1838).
National Library of Australia:
nla.pic-an2818282.

Just six weeks later, Ann Cowper ushered her four, newly acquired step-children onto the *Indispensable*, in company with some 62 female prisoners. On 2 March, Captain Henry Best set sail. The *Indispensable* parson was on his way, and the parish of Sydney awaited.

The Plan of God to redeem the world, which had fired his vision as a boy, and which was fuelled by the Evangelicals at Hull, now smouldered quietly in expectation of great things to come.

2 | From Rebellion to Royal Commission
(1809–1821) | Vision Builds Society

William Cowper left his homeland as a warrior sets out for a battlefield. It is likely that John Downame's *The Christian Warfare* occupied his attention on the long journey to NSW. As he stepped ashore in August 1809, the struggle for the soul of his new land began. God's vision had a society to build.

The colony was in disarray. Since the overthrow of Governor Bligh on 26 January 1808, the rebels had ruled the land. Acting Governor William Paterson advised his new chaplain to 'regard every man as rogue until he found him to be an honest man'.

The parish of St Phillip had been proclaimed on 23 July 1802, but it was only on Sunday 20 August 1809 that it received its first clergyman. Like Richard Johnson before him, Cowper was soon rumoured to be 'a Methodist'. A Government Order proclaimed that he would be stationed here 'until further orders'. Cowper stayed for the rest of his days.

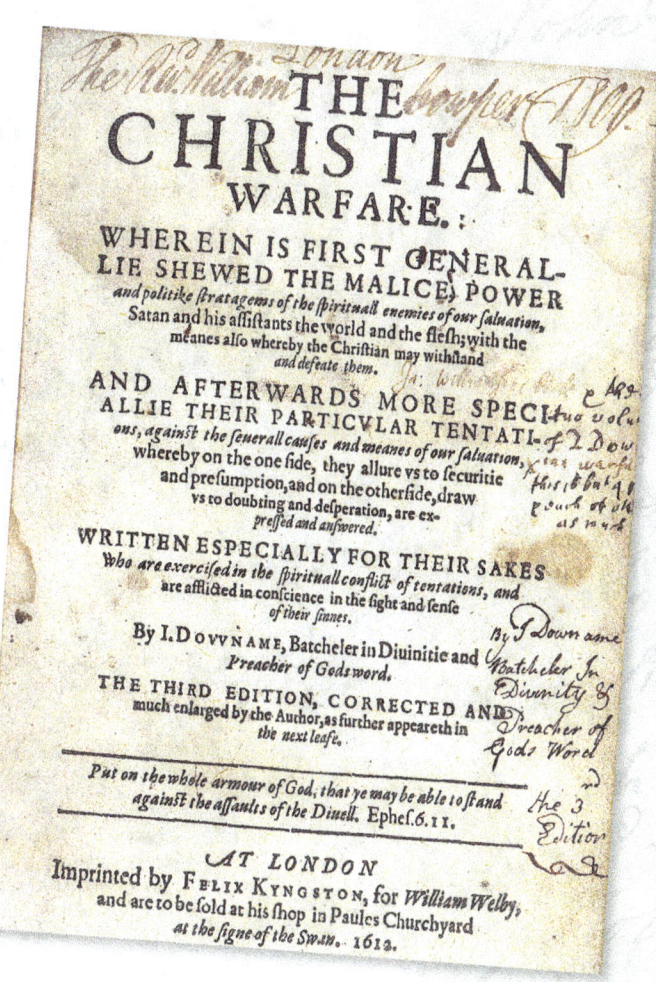

Title page from William Cowper's copy of John Downame, *Christian Warfare*, 1612 edition. Courtesy & Photo: Tim Cowper.

The *Indispensable* rested at anchor in Sydney Cove alongside another ship, the *Boyd*, which had arrived four days earlier. As the *Indispensable* parson became a member of the Committee of the Female Orphan School, and conducted the marriage of William Gaudry—the first of hundreds more and an anticipation of a long campaign to redress the colony's reluctance to participate in that institution—the *Boyd* prepared to sail for New Zealand.

Lachlan Macquarie arrived to resume the government on 1 January 1810. The period of rebellion was over, and life in Sydney was about to become more settled. Governor and Chaplain began to institute the structures necessary to build a civilized society. Early orders were issued urging people to marry, to observe the Sabbath, to send their children to school.

As one of the first things to happen on arrival, the postmaster would board to receive the mail. St Phillip's can be seen to the left of Nichols.

Stamp, copied, Australia [four pence] Isaac Nichols [first post master] boarding ship in Sydney, 1809, 1959. National Archives of Australia: C4078, N12078.

The Cowpers moved into the Johnson's old parsonage, one of a row of four houses for government officials in Bridge Street. Here, on 27 July

Major Johnson announcing the arrest of Governor Bligh, 1928. Raymond Lindsay. Oil on canvas. Geelong Gallery. Gift of Dame Nellie Melba, 1928. © Estate of the artist.

Requisition to Major Johnson to assume control of the colony, 26 Jan 1808. State Library of NSW: ML Safe 4/5.

1810, William and Ann's only child, William Macquarie, was born—William's future biographer. This was the son who followed in his father's ministerial footsteps, eventually becoming the first Dean of Sydney and serving even longer in the ministry than his father. When William died and 'Mac' was appointed as his replacement at St Philip's, it became what is still the only father-son succession in any parish in Sydney. Mac's early memories included eating oranges from the trees planted by the first Chaplain.

The rebellion had left the Colony with many inner tensions that required some mending. One directly affected the new parson. When Marsden had left for England, Henry Fulton, a clergyman who had come to NSW as a convict but then pardoned, had been left to do duty in his place. Fulton was already unhappy with the financial arrangements Marsden had made for him, but his feelings grew worse when he remained loyal to Bligh during the rebellion, but felt unsupported in this action. When Cowper arrived as Marsden's recruit, Fulton resented his presence and wrote home with some hasty judgements about the newcomer.

If the colony was to be rebuilt for the future, long-term strategies were required. Early in 1810, Cowper assisted the Kissing Point School Master so that he could resume taking pupils. By April, the new Charity school under Cowper's direction called for pupils, and appointed Mr John Davies as teacher. Macquarie urged the citizens of NSW to build school houses, just like the settlers at Liverpool had done in 1811. In 1812 St Philip's opened its Parochial School.

St Philip's Church of England Schools plaque, St Philip's Sydney. Courtesy: St Philip's. Photo: Peter Bolt.

These were the beginnings of Cowper's life-long interest in education. In the midst of his many pastoral responsibilities, he personally educated his own sons. Cowper's role on the committee of the Female Orphan School was especially important, since further initiatives in education grew out of this institution. Across the years, he was instrumental in establishing schools at the primary and secondary levels, and from the late twenties he was also part of a group seeking to establish Australia's first college for tertiary study.

In February 1810, Senior Chaplain Marsden returned from England, bringing another recruit to be his second Assistant Chaplain, Robert Cartwright, who was placed at the Hawkesbury. Marsden also brought

Bridge Street can be seen going up the picture on the right. In the group of four houses on the right of it, the Parsonage was the second.

View of part of the river of Sydney, in New South Wales. Taken from St Phillip's church yard, 1813. Unknown artist. National Gallery of Australia, Canberra.

CHAPTER 2 | FROM REBELLION TO ROYAL COMMISSION (1809–1821)

William Hall and John King, 'lay settlers', whom he had recruited to begin the work of the Church Missionary Society in New Zealand. However, when they stepped ashore, Sydney was still reeling from the news that the entire crew of the *Boyd* had been killed and eaten by the New Zealanders. It would be four years before the Governor considered it safe enough for the missionaries to sail.

As further reports filtered back about the *Boyd*, it became clear that the crew had met their grizzly fate as a reprisal for abuse suffered by some New Zealanders who had sailed on the *Boyd*. Being aware of a growing number of similar cases of the mistreatment of indigenous populations at the hands of Europeans in the South Seas, the Chaplains took up the cause of the victims. Marsden's agitation with the Governor and the public led to a bond being levied from vessels leaving Sydney, which was forfeit in case of any crimes inflicted amongst the islands. Since the abuse often began on shipboard, in December 1813 the 'New South Wales Philanthropic Society, for the Protection and Civilization of such of the Natives of the South Seas who may arrive at Port Jackson' came into existence, with William Cowper on the Special Committees for Protection and Accounts.

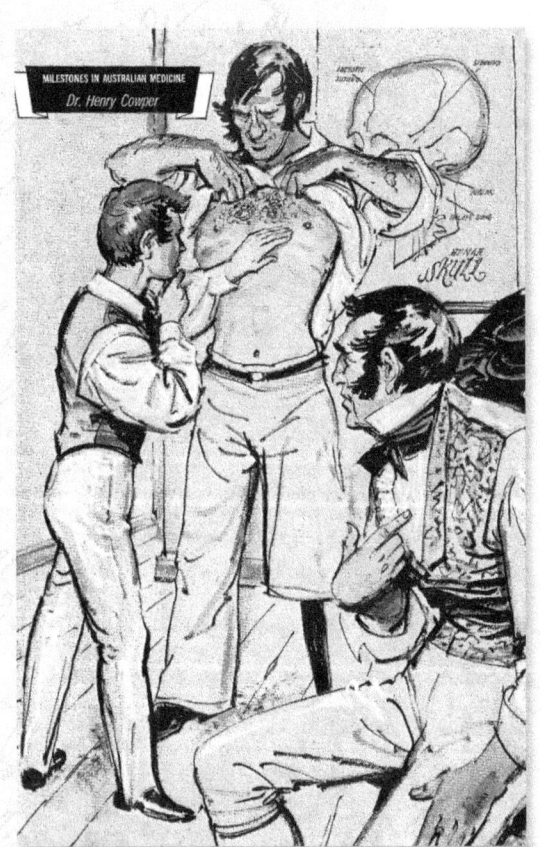

Henry Cowper examining a Patient under the supervision of William Redfern, one of the series of postcards, 'Milestones in Medicine', by Parke-Davis (now Pfizer). Used by Permission.

This was to be a decade of the formation of new philanthropic societies, the oldest of which had been formed a few months earlier. The 'New South Wales Society for Promoting Christian Knowledge and Benevolence in These Territories and in the Neighbouring Islands' came into existence on 8 May 1813, to relieve the distressed of NSW, protect the natives of the neighbouring islands, and assist the work of the Tahitian mission. The broad focus of the initial aims made it difficult to gain the support of Governor and Chaplains. After narrowing the focus to the relief of the distressed of NSW, subscriptions increased, Macquarie subscribed, and in 1816–17 William Cowper joined the committee. In June 1818, the name was changed to match the narrower focus: the Benevolent Society of NSW.

After the New Zealand mission began at the end of 1814, Cowper often found himself with extra responsibility, when his Senior Chaplain was visiting the missionaries. Even at this early stage of his life in NSW, his health had begun to suffer. About three years after his arrival, he was afflicted with a severe bout of rheumatic fever, said to be brought on by his visitation of condemned prisoners in the damp gaol cells. Although Doctors Wentworth and Redfern feared for him, his recovery eventually came—even if he suffered severe pains for many years afterwards.

Hoping for a little more security for his growing family, William requested some land. In June 1811, he received 600 acres in the district of Cooke. He slowly amassed cattle enough to supply 4,000 lbs meat to the Government stores early in 1818. If the land was for any potential farmers amongst his four sons, things soon took a different turn for his eldest. In July 1814, fourteen year old Henry was 'apprenticed' (without indenture) to William Redfern to learn the surgeon's trade and, in 1816 he became the first clinical assistant at the magnificent new General Hospital in Macquarie Street.

(Old) St Philip's Church. J. Lewin. State Library of NSW: PXD 388 V.1 f.7.

While Marsden was in New Zealand getting the CMS mission established, thoughts turned to the 'civilization' of the indigenous peoples of NSW. At the end of 1814, Macquarie established a Native Institution at Parramatta, 'for the Education of the Native Children of both sexes'. Cowper served on the committee—an early expression of his life-long pledge 'never to abandon the poor despised aboriginal'.

By 1815, St Philip's was already overcrowded. Those holding tickets-of-leave were asked to come in the afternoon, not the morning. The end of the Napoleonic Wars meant increasing numbers of both settlers and convicts were coming to NSW. The work of Sydney's parish clergyman had been steadily growing along with the town's population. Cowper had had several assistants: Fulton (1812–1814), the controversial Benjamin Vale (1814–1816), and from June 1819, Richard Hill. After the number of Sunday Services at St Philip's had been increased, the next step was the formation of the parish of St James. When the building was completed in 1821, Hill was installed as the incumbent, leaving Cowper, once again, on his own.

Lachlan Macquarie, 1822. Richard Read snr. (ca. 1765–1827?). State Library of NSW: P2/144.

CHAPTER 2 | FROM REBELLION TO ROYAL COMMISSION (1809–1821)

THE
FIRST REPORT
OF THE
Auxiliary Bible Society
OF
NEW SOUTH WALES.
1817.
WITH A LIST OF
BENEFACTORS & SUBSCRIBERS.
SYDNEY:
PRINTED BY G. HOWE.

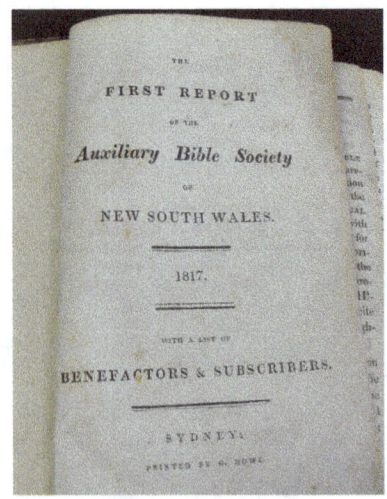

Title page of *The First Report of the Auxiliary Bible Society of NSW* (1817). Courtesy: NSW Bible Society. Photo: John Cowper.

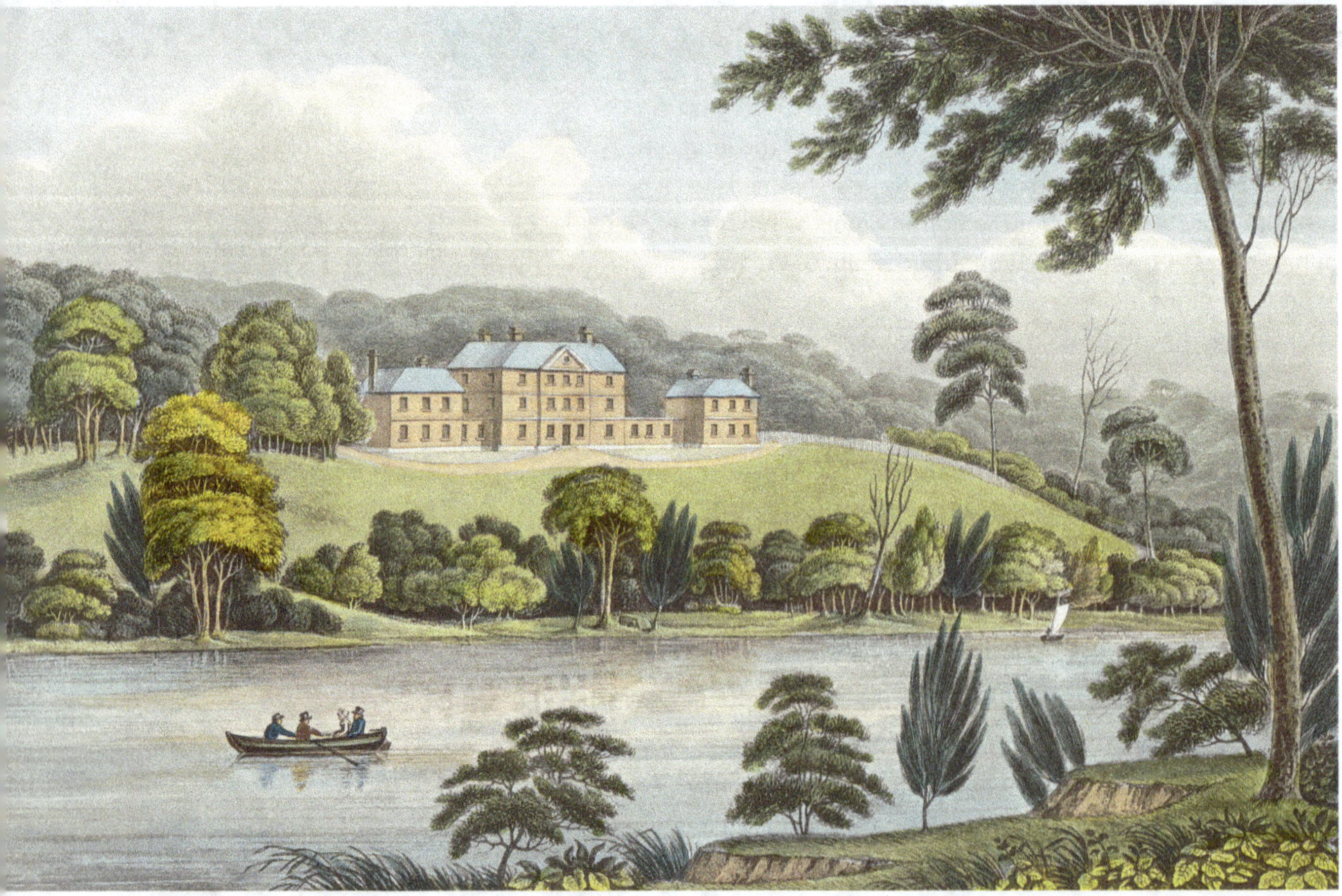

NSW was rapidly becoming more than a penal Colony, and Macquarie saw that a larger vision was also required. Social policy had to include the steadily growing number of ex-convicts, despite the ill-feeling this aroused in some quarters. The British Government saw no need for a penal colony to have a bank, or its own currency, but Macquarie was well aware of the problems that this had caused, and saw the need for both. In November 1816, William Cowper was amongst those called together to talk about how to fix wages and the price of labour, given the amount of Sterling circulating in the Colony. Reforms to the Currency and the establishment of the Bank of New South Wales soon followed.

At a public meeting in March 1817, a local Auxiliary of the British and Foreign Bible Society was formed, with William Cowper and Edward Riley joint secretaries. William Macquarie Cowper, although just short of seven at the time, remembered his father coming home, 'as glad as though he had found a great treasure'. At the same meeting, the Governor proposed a second institution to look into the founding of schools, in which children would learn to read the Bible. Thus Cowper also found himself on The Provisional Committee for the Institution of Public Schools.

The Bible Society Committee was an active committee, with members involved in door to door visitation in order to ascertain which households of the Colony did not have a Bible, so that one might be offered. This visitation unearthed a great deal of poverty and hardship throughout the Colony. On 6 May 1818, 'an Association for the Relief

View of the Female Orphan School near Parramatta, New South Wales, 1825. Joseph Lycett (ca. 1775–1828). National Library of Australia: nla.pic-an7690892.

of the Poor, Aged and Infirm, and for other Benevolent Purposes' was formed, with Cowper on its committee.

In June 1818, the Female Orphan Institute moved to new premises at Parramatta, and immediately plans were made for a Male Orphan School to begin in the vacated buildings. Both Schools operated under the same Committee, and, from this base further initiatives for the education of 'the rising generation' were emerging. The Chaplains were asked to nominate names of boys to begin at the new school.

Cowper delayed his answer, while, in August 1818, he accompanied Lachlan and Elizabeth Macquarie to Newcastle. Despite William suffering on board from violent seasickness, and Ann suffering at home from rumours that some escaped convicts were waiting to pirate the ship, Newcastle's first visit from a clergyman was a success, and Cowper busied himself with performing many overdue baptisms and marriages.

An important development in education occurred in 1820, when the quarterly General Committee for the two Orphan Schools created an operating Committee that would henceforth meet weekly. From this point onwards, oversight of the schools fell mainly on Cowper, his colleague Richard Hill, and Henry Antill. A sub-committee was asked to report on the colony's schools. Questionnaires were circulated to the various masters, and by January 1821 the report was submitted. The report should have been of use to Rev. Thomas Reddall, who had recently arrived to introduce the Madras System of education. He took twelve boys from the Male Orphan School to his new school at Macquarie Fields, where they were also joined by the sons of Governor Macquarie and Lieut.-Governor Sorrell (Van Diemen's Land).

Elizabeth Macquarie, Miniature.
State Library of NSW: MIN 70.

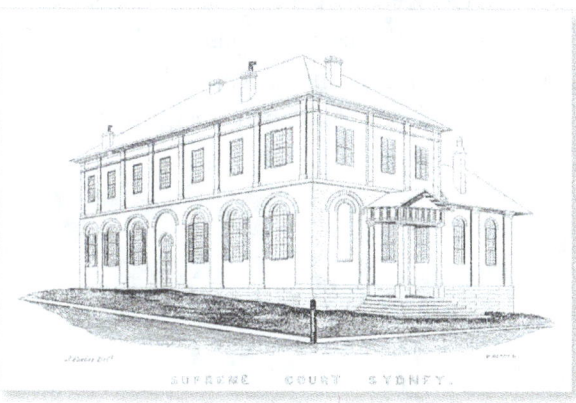

At the end of March, 1820, the foundation of 'the Georgian Public School' was laid near Hyde Park. The news of the King's death in January had not yet reached the colony, and when Cowper addressed the crowd on the importance of education, he noted that King George III, 'in the days of his health', had frequently expressed the desire that every poor child in his dominion should be able to learn to read the Bible. The school was never opened, and the buildings became the Supreme Court of NSW.

LEFT: The Georgian School never opened. Its building was used for the Supreme Court.

Supreme Court, Sydney, 1848. Print, engraving. Joseph Fowles (1810–1878). From *Sydney in 1848* (Sydney: J. Fowles, 1849).

In July 1820, Macquarie read the proclamation that George IV was the only right and proper king of NSW. This same month Thomas Cowper, freshly turned 18 and 'having been 2 ½ years employed for his own benefit', requested a piece of the new King's territory. Although probably regarded as a 'currency kid', he requested the same rights as a new settler to be granted him. By August he was given these rights, 300 acres, four cows, and victuals for himself and three government men for 6 months. In September, his older brother Henry also received four cows from the Government herds, but without any land of his own, the young doctor probably kept them on the grants of his father or his brother Thomas.

Unlike Johnson or Marsden before him, or even his contemporary, Cartwright, Cowper consistently refused to act as a magistrate. He had come to the colony to fight a Christian Warfare. He refused the magistracy on the biblical principle 'no man that warreth entangles himself with the affairs of life' (2 Timothy 2:4). His greatest weapon in this struggle was his devotion to his duties as the parson.

But sometimes his civic responsibilities worked in favour of his convictions as a Christian minister. In 1819 he clashed with Government officials over the licensing of publicans. As he debated who should get a licence, Cowper's playful sense of humour shows a man who is confident of his own views and assured of his valued position in society.

Refusal of the magistracy did not mean that Cowper lacked social concern. His understanding of the Christian warfare led him to be involved with a range of societies set up for the good of the colony. Time and again, he displayed a vision for the future coupled with practical steps towards its realisation. On 31 July 1819, for example, William donated a cow to the Benevolent Society, for the purpose of creating a fund, which would provide an Asylum for the Aged and Infirm. After providing for its beginnings, Cowper worked on the Committee that saw the Asylum open in October 1821. In August 1819, he was involved in a further initiative to reach the indigenous population, as the 'New South Wales Society for Promoting Christian Knowledge amongst the Aborigines of New South Wales and its Dependencies' was formed.

A view of the west side of Sydney cove, [c.1803]. Attributed to George William Evans. State Library of NSW: DG V1/73.

August 1819 was also the month when Cowper stood in George Street, amongst the moderate crowd gathered to witness the laying of a foundation stone for St Andrew's Cathedral. However, almost as soon as it began, the work was stopped by Commissioner J.T. Bigge.

The Benevolent Asylum can be seen to the right of the Toll Gate.

Toll Gate and Benevolent Asylum, George Street South, [1836]. Robert Russell (1808–1900). State Library of NSW: Original: PXA 581/7.

Bigge arrived in September 1819, accompanied by his secretary (and his sister's brother-in-law) Thomas Hobbes Scott. He had been appointed to make an extensive inquiry into the Colony of NSW, as part of the review of the effectiveness of Transportation. Macquarie's public expenditure and his liberal policy on emancipated convicts also came under investigation. Bigge was full of praise for the diligence of all of the Chaplains. On Cowper, Bigge observed that 'he has always paid the most unremitting attention to his clerical duties' and noted 'his extensive charitable occupations' (Bigge, I.143). Bigge's report would prove to be unfairly critical of Macquarie, and so, when the Commissioner left the colony in 1821, the Macquarie era was about to come to an end. His departure also brought another change for the Cowper family. On 14 February Henry, almost 21 years old, left for England on the *Dromedary* with Bigge and Scott, to face examination before the Royal College of Surgeons. Henry had had a troubled time in Sydney. At the end of 1821, when Macquarie also returned, William asked him to see what he could do to find Henry a medical position in England.

Cowper had been with Macquarie from the beginning. They arrived to a colony in rebellion and, by the time Macquarie left, many foundations had been laid for a new society. The humanitarian Governor had fought his battles, but was recalled before he saw the realisation of his vision. The Chaplain, ever engaged in his Christian Warfare, remained. There was still plenty more for him to see.

3 | Two Archdeacons and a Bishop
(1821–1842) | Vision Regulates Life

*W*HEN MACQUARIE WAS about to depart, a public meeting failed to gain unanimity over an address to farewell their departing Governor, and one to welcome his successor, Thomas Brisbane. At the handover on 1 December, 1821, Macquarie spoke with some feeling about his enemies, and about 'base calumny, vindictive slander, and malicious reproach'. He also spoke of the vast improvement of the colony under his direction, confident that this would bring 'the applause of Posterity'.

North View of Sydney New South Wales, 1822. Joseph Lycett (ca. 1775–1828). State Library of NSW: DG v1/11.

Annual Meeting of the NSW Auxiliary Bible Society, 14 August 1821	
Distributed since last meeting:	
Bibles	524
Testaments	374
Distributed since inauguration of NSW Auxiliary:	
Bibles	1514
Testaments	1974
Total	3488

Source: Sydney Gazette 18 August 1821.

William Cowper had no reason not to sign Macquarie's farewell address. Already in the public mind, as in posterity, the two men were closely associated in their concern for reform. They, with many others, had worked together to establish structures and institutions for even greater improvement of NSW society. Macquarie, from his humanitarian concerns; and Cowper from his vision of God's Redemptive plan.

In 1821, Sydney continued to grow, and the Christian ministry was growing apace. In April, an additional evening service was added at St Philip's, the Annual Meeting of the Bible Society heard that five local branches had been formed, and a total of 3,488 Bibles had been distributed, and Macquarie divided Sydney into two parishes, St Philip's to the north of King Street, and St James to the south.

The pressure was being felt by Sydney's parson. As Macquarie was about to leave, William resigned from the Orphan and Native Schools Committees, and Ann withdrew from being the patroness of the Female Orphan School. They cited domestic reasons, with William admitting that his health had become 'so much impaired', that he wished 'to devote the little strength [he had] to the Clerical Duties' of his very populous parish.

By the twenties, Cowper's ministry had settled into a regular pattern. His parish duties were onerous enough, with preaching and prayers at Sunday Services, the pastoral visitation which so endeared him to the townsfolk, including visitation of prisoners in the gaol, which often brought the terrible duty of attending at their execution. He was also in demand to act as an examiner or speaker at the annual meetings of the regular weekday Schools, such as the Orphan Institutions, or the Macquarie Street Academy; and also those of the Sunday Schools, such as that at Parramatta and, in time, those opened by the Wesleyans.

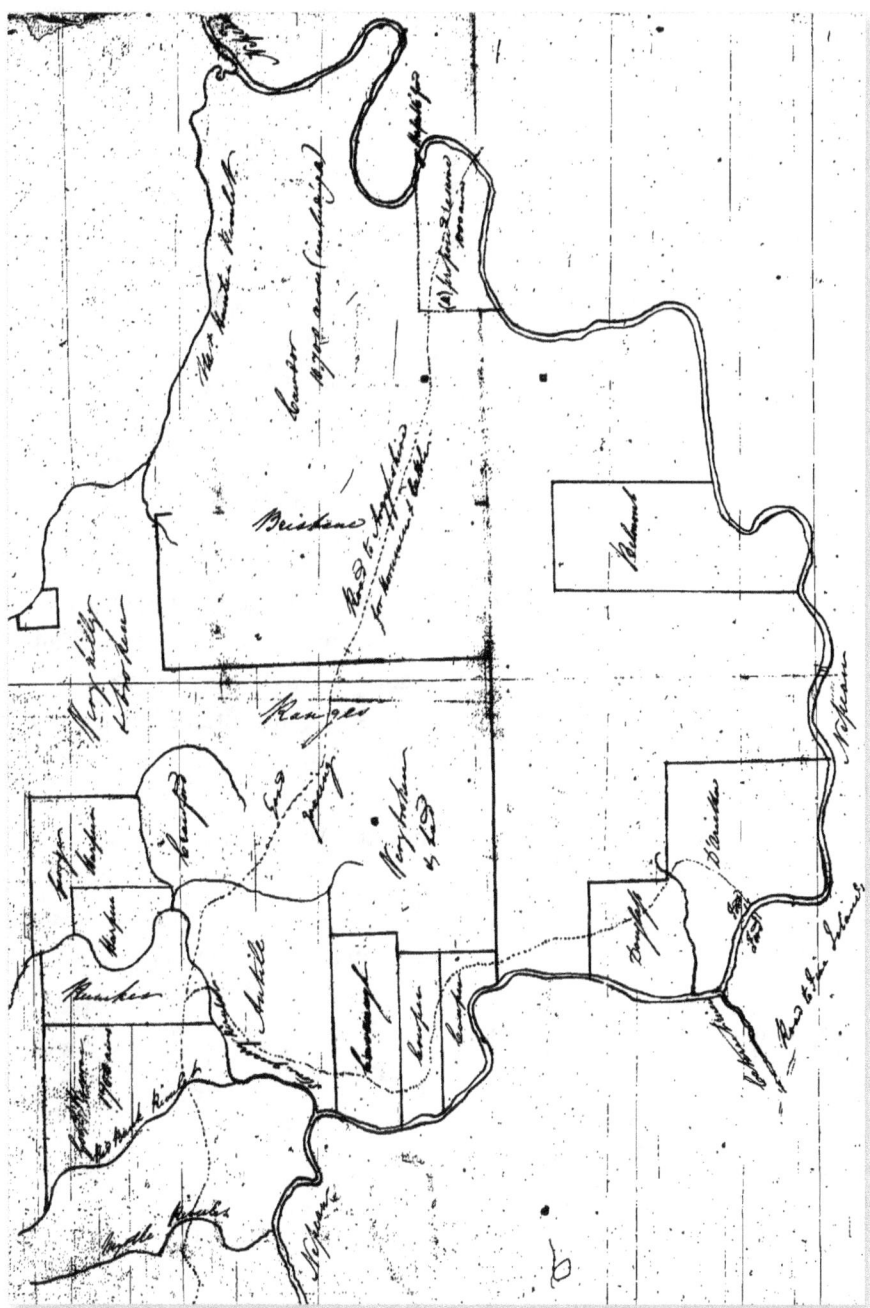

The two Cowper properties can be seen bottom centre.

Map of the Cowpastures, 29 Jan 1823. Mitchell Library: Macarthur Papers, Vol. 66, A2962, 119.

His children were now entering the adult world. Thomas was actively farming, receiving cattle from the Government and convicts to care for them. By January 1825, he requested the occupation of a run in Burragorang, since the 220 cows in his care were overloading the two Cowper properties in the Cowpastures—170 branded to William, 40 to Thomas. Although he received the ticket, he handed it back at the end of the same year, also requesting a grant the size allowed free settlers, namely 2000 acres. He already had 500 and was given 500 more just before Thomas Brisbane sailed.

In September 1822, Henry 'overcame the greatest trial [he had] ever experienced' when he became the first 'New Hollander' to face the

CHAPTER 3 | TWO ARCHDEACONS AND A BISHOP (1821–1842)

Henry Cowper to William Cowper, 16 Sept 1822. Keith Cowper Family Archive.

Royal College of Surgeons examination—passing with credit. Although he could see himself staying in England, he arrived back in Sydney on 31 May 1823 and, after practicing medicine in Parramatta for a time, in September 1825 he became the Surgeon-in-Charge of the hospital at the new settlement of Moreton Bay.

Mary, too, was blossoming into a young woman. In January 1825, 10 cows in Thomas's problematically large herd bore the brand of his twenty year old sister. She was also beginning to take a part in some of the social institutions being established in the colony. The Female School of Industry was established in March 1826, and, by May, it had been placed in the 'immediate care' of Mary, step-mother Ann, and Mrs Wemyss. Mary was also conspicuous amongst the ladies involved with the Auxiliary Bible Society. On 2 September 1828, William had the joy of officiating at Mary's marriage to George Brooks, Surgeon at Newcastle. As a wedding present from the government, Mary was granted 1,280 acres in the Newcastle District.

Female School of Industry, 1832. William Wilson. National Gallery of Australia, Canberra.

In February 1827, sixteen year old William Macquarie sailed for England, a parting which Ann spoke of as 'a very great trial to us'. Apparently, even more than his mother did, father William 'felt the separation very much indeed'. Nevertheless, Ann hoped that it would benefit him and many others. Mac prepared for the ministry, first with Rev. Glubb at Dartmouth, and then by graduating M.A. at Oxford. When he returned in 1836, he held the honour of being the first Australian-born clergyman. The letters William wrote to his youngest son while he was in England are filled with news, advice about what to read, exhortations, and expressions of fatherly affection.

In February 1823, William's ill-health apparently made him, once again, somewhat anxious about his own future, and so his family's security. In view of 'the present precarious state of his health' he requested Earl Bathurst, through Commissioner Bigge, to grant him a pension on his retirement that might continued to be paid to his widow in the event of his death.

His concerns about the future did not curb his vision for taking the gospel to his new land. On 23 December 1822 Cowper chaired the meeting that founded the Sydney Bethel Union Society, which aimed at procuring a place of worship for seamen, like the 'floating chapel' on the Thames, or a 'spot of Ground, contiguous to the Shipping'. In August 1823, Cowper was involved with the commencement of a NSW Auxiliary of the Religious Tract Society, which immediately made rapid progress. Their third annual meeting (September, 1826) heard that 62,822 Tracts had been distributed in the previous 12 months, by the 5th (1828) they had distributed a total of 98,939.

When the London Missionary Society deputation (Tyerman and Bennet) visited from August 1824 into 1825, they were appalled at how little had been done for the indigenous people. Very keen that something should begin, Cowper offered them advice. In January 1824, he had already written to Samuel Leigh, urging that a Wesleyan mission to the Aboriginals might be opened at the new settlement at Moreton Bay. When Lancelot Threlkeld began his translation work amongst the Awabakal people at Lake Macquarie, William Cowper was one of his active, financial supporters, and he also helped him get his work published. In 1827 at the 7th Annual meeting of the Sydney Bible Association, with Cowper in the Chair, Threlkeld spoke passionately about his hopes for success, denying the common view that these people 'represented a mere connecting link between the human and brute creation'.

In January-February 1825, an Auxiliary of the Church Missionary Society was established, in response to 'the late alarming and fatal contests which have occurred between the Aborigines and Europeans' and the expansion of settlement to Port Macquarie and Moreton Bay. This was in the belief that missionary activity amongst the Aboriginals would prevent further troubles and loss of life. As a clergyman, Cowper was automatically a committee member and, after colleague Richard

Estimate of the charge of defraying the Civil

Civil Establishment of NSW from 1/1/1824 to 31/12/1824:[1]

	£	s	d
Governor	2500		
Lieut. Governor	450		
Judge	2000		
Attorney General	600		
Provost Marshall	91	5	
Surveyor of Lands	365		
Assistant	250		
2nd Assistant	200		
3rd Assistant	150		
Chaplain	350		
1st Assistant	260		
2nd Assistant	240		
3rd Assistant	182	10	

1. Estimate of defraying the Civil Establishment, 1 Jan 1824 (Col.Sec. 6059, 4/1774, 5a–b).

The Bethel Flag.
From http://www.sydneybethelunion.com.au.
Used by Permission Sydney Bethel Union.

Native of New South Wales from Wellington Valley, 1826. Augustus Earle (1793–1838). National Library of Australia: nla.pic-an2818346.

Hill died in 1836, he would take over as Secretary for many years. The first quarterly meeting, held in April 1825, discussed 'plans and suggestions for the improvement of the Aborigines'. CMS received a grant of 10,000 acres of land for this mission, and when William Watson and Johann Handt arrived in 1832 as its first missionaries, the Wellington Valley Mission had begun.

Besides fostering a concern for mission, the eighteenth century Evangelical Revival had sparked a whole range of societies working for reform. Evangelicals such as Elizabeth Fry had placed prison reform on the wider agenda for both politicians and churchmen, and it was natural for the Chaplains in the penal colony of NSW to keep an interest. 1825 was apparently the year for William Cowper to pursue such matters more actively. After reading something in the *Quarterly Review*, in August he sent some suggestions for Prison Discipline to Sherriff Mackaness. By the year's end, he had sat on boards of inquiry into the women's prison at Emu Plains, Carter's Barracks, and the Female Factory.

At this time, Cowper had just received a new superior. On 7 May 1825, Thomas Hobbes Scott, Commissioner Bigge's secretary, began his brief and turbulent second tour of NSW, but now in a new role. After he had returned home in 1821, he had taken Holy Orders and the parish of Whitfield, in the Diocese of Durham. He had also submitted a proposal to the Government for the establishment of an education system for NSW. On the strength of this, Scott was sent back as Australia's first Archdeacon. With the arrival of Scott, the Anglican Church in NSW was becoming more regularised.

Footstone of the grave of Thomas Hobbes Scott. St John's Whitfield. Photo: Peter Bolt.

On 9 June 1825, Scott summoned his clergy to St James for his Primary Visitation, and just six months later, in January 1826, he gathered them again. This time they met to form a District Committee of the *Society for Promoting Christian Knowledge*, in order to assist in the circulation of Religious Books—regarded as a key instrument of social improvement.

In March 1826 a new Corporation for Clergy and School Lands was formed, with all the Chaplains as members, to manage one seventh of the lands of the colony, now granted for the Church of England and for education. The day after his nineteenth birthday, William's third son, Charles, was appointed the Clerk of the Corporation. After his first job with the Commissary's Department, this was another step towards his later political career. The Corporation immediately began instituting Scott's plans for improving education, which would leave the colony with more schools, the beginnings of secondary education, teacher-training centres, and mechanics institutes, although the Corporation itself was doomed to close down in 1833.

The Societies and institutions already established now had their weekly, monthly and annual patterns, which also added routine to Cowper's duties, and still more institutions were yet to come into existence. In March 1826, the Gentlemen of the city, including Reverend Cowper, concerned about their own moral improvement, opened the Australian Subscription Library and Reading Room—a forerunner of the State Library of NSW.

By the mid twenties, times were tough for many people in Sydney. In October 1826, the Benevolent Society reported that they 'have been for some time wholly without Funds', and the Chaplains were invited to preach charity sermons on behalf of this organisation. The particular concern that Sydney's poor could not afford medical treatment led to the founding of the Sydney Dispensary in June 1826, with Cowper on the Committee.

Australian Subscription Library, 1848. Joseph Fowles (1810–1878). From *Sydney in 1848* (Sydney: J. Fowles, 1849).

The Dispensary is the long building to the left.

Hyde Park, St James Parsonage Dispensary, afterwards the Mint, and Emigration Barracks, 1842. John Rae. State Library of NSW: DG.

CHAPTER 3 | TWO ARCHDEACONS AND A BISHOP (1821–1842)

Major Mitchell sketching the entrance of the caves in Wellington Valley, New South Wales, 1843. William Romaine Govett (1807–1848). National Library of Australia: nla.pic-an4700786.

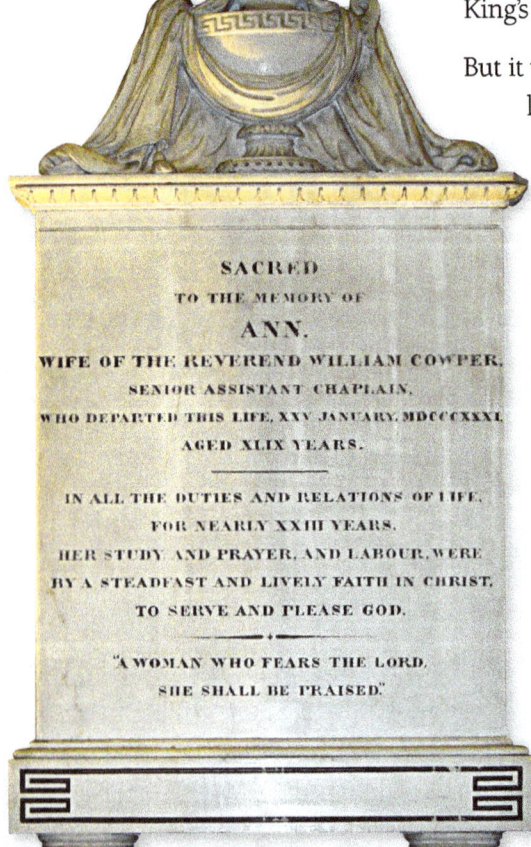

Ann Cowper (nee Barrell) memorial, St Philip's Sydney. Courtesy: St Philip's. Photo: Peter Bolt.

In September 1829, even before Scott left the colony, his successor, William Grant Broughton, arrived. He found William Cowper in a very poor state of health, with his doctors advising that he be relieved from duties. Cowper went to the country for a short time, but, missing his parishioners, he soon returned to active duty. By January 1830, Cowper was well enough to assist the Corporation launch a plan for the foundation of two Grammar Schools feeding into the colony's first tertiary institution. This plan eventually led to the formation of The King's Schools and Moore College.

But it was not William's poor health that struck him with tragedy a year later. On 24 January 1831, Ann Cowper attended church on Sunday as normal. On Monday, however, she 'was attacked with a violent indisposition', and by Tuesday night she had died. The *Gazette* noted that many would remember her for her piety and many virtues. On 6 February William preached a sermon that produced public accolades, and when he spoke about her virtues every eye was upon him and the congregation listened with great sympathy for their beloved pastor. On 3 July —her absent son's twenty-first birthday—William sat down and wrote to him. He remembered how peaceful she looked the day before her burial—a sign of the heavenly bliss she was now enjoying, while he described himself as 'yet a mourner'. From England, Archdeacon Scott shipped a marble tablet in her memory to be erected in St Philip's.

October 1831 brought another changeover in Government, as Governor Darling left the colony—taking his eldest son, whom William had tutored for two hours each morning. Perhaps this boy had reminded the grieving father of his own greatly missed 'scholar', then about to enter Oxford University.

As Cowper continued to mourn Ann's death, his 1832 literary productivity was perhaps therapeutic. Impressed by the Christian Faith expressed by a little girl, Margaret Gold, as she died, William wrote up her story as a tract. This, in turn, led to him publishing another tract about Mrs Susanna Day, a friend of Ann, who had also died expressing a strong Christian Faith. Both tracts sold well and by October William was talking of second editions.

1832 was an occasion for great rejoicing for CMS, and for Cowper in particular. In a rather buoyant letter to his son, he gave thanks for the arrival of William Watson 'to commence a Mission to the Blacks' at Wellington Valley, joined later in the year by Johann Handt. The mission made a good start, and in the following year Watson brought an Aboriginal boy, Goongeen, to Sydney, where he was greatly delighted when William Cowper played the organ for his amusement.

In March 1834, Archdeacon Broughton sailed for England to promote the interests of the Church in NSW and, on 14 February 1836 he found himself appointed the first (and only) Bishop of Australia.

William Macquarie Cowper took advantage of the Archdeacon being in England. In 1835 he consulted him about his future, but Broughton was unable to assure the young man of a position in NSW. When Mac arrived in Sydney on 16 February 1836, it was therefore as Chaplain for the Australian Agricultural Company, bound for twenty years of ministry at Stroud. Mac's new wife Margaret was delighted to meet her father-in-law, who had his own domestic news to report. After being widowed now for five years, William had proposed to Harriette Swaine,

BELOW RIGHT: *Portrait of Harriette Swaine,* [before 1833]. Keith Cowper Family Archive.

BELOW LEFT: *Portrait of the Late Right Rev. W. Broughton, Bishop of Sydney, &c,* 1857. Walter G. Mason. National Library of Australia: nla.pic-an7978975.

CHAPTER 3 | TWO ARCHDEACONS AND A BISHOP (1821–1842)

a twenty-seven year old, who had arrived on 17 December 1833 from Wisbech, Cambridgeshire, aboard the *Layton*. On 1 March 1836 they married at St Philip's. It was the season for Cowper marriages. In 1837, William's son Henry, who had returned to Sydney from Moreton Bay in January 1833, married Eliza Prince, the governess of the Hassall children, and an excellent teacher. In 1838, Henry acquired land in the County of Murray, and the pair moved to Bungonia, where Henry practiced medicine.

When Broughton arrived back in NSW to be installed on 5 June 1836, the Anglican Church entered a new stage of its history. The day before his consecration, he was presented with an address, in which the new Episcopal See was proclaimed as yet another example of His Majesty's paternal watchfulness over his Dominions, and of the pre-eminence of the English nation. Broughton immediately formed a *Diocesan* Committee of the Society for the Promotion of Christian Knowledge/Society for the Promulgation of the Gospel, and Cowper became joint secretary with Sheriff McQuoid. This committee was to have a special concern for new churches and schools, and, in January 1837, all chaplains were invited to preach sermons in favour of the objects of the committee.

Rev'd Dr William Cowper, senior chaplain of New South Wales. Unknown artist. Pencil Portrait, after Read. State Library of NSW: PXA 972/4.

In July 1836, the Bishop chaired a meeting of Protestants, who formed themselves into a committee to gather support for a petition to the Legislative Council objecting to Governor Bourke's policy of General Education based on the Irish system. William Cowper, William Macquarie, and Charles were all involved at their various local chapters of this 'Protestant Committee'. Eventually the combination of the Church and the Dissenters defeated Bourke's bill, leaving the thorny issue of a General Education System to his successors.

This was also the time of a rising Temperance movement. In September 1836 the second annual meeting of the fledgling NSW Temperance Society heard that it already had eight or nine hundred members. William Cowper addressed the meeting, and the press reported that the mood in favour of the total prohibition of spirits was becoming very prevalent. The use of spirits in NSW had a long and chequered past, and an effective solution to its problems had to be found for a better future to be realised. Perhaps the birth of Elizabeth Ann, on 19 December 1836, added extra incentive to Cowper's vision of an improved society, as he dreamed of a better future for his children, and for the children of others.

With Australia's own Bishop, further regularisation of the Anglican Church was now possible. In November, 1836, Cowper was appointed as Broughton's Commissary and in December he was appointed Surrogate for granting licences of Marriage. In December, Bishop Broughton also conducted the first Australian ordination—that of Rev. Thomas Sharpe. With a Bishop now in Sydney, it was appropriate to give him a seat, and so the building of the Cathedral, previously stopped by Commissioner Bigge, was restarted. On 16 May 1837, the Governor laid the foundation stone for St Andrew's Cathedral in the middle of the day, school children performed in the afternoon, and a dinner with speeches extended long into the evening.

Portrait of William Cowper, 1833. R. Read. State Library of NSW: P2/236.

At the end of 1837, on 5 December, Governor Richard Bourke left the Colony. After receiving addresses from a variety of groups of citizens and holding a final levee at Government House, he embarked to the cheers of an adoring crowd and the firing of artillery. His successor, George Gipps arrived on 24 February 1838.

In the middle of the Colony's Jubilee year, 1838, Samuel Marsden, William's oldest colleague and friend in the ministry died. The departure of this pioneering missionary chaplain marked the end of an era. His efforts lay behind so many of the initiatives which had enabled ministry and societal institutions to become firmly established as part of the colony's regular life. His death also meant that, at least in terms of length of service, Cowper was now the most senior clergyman, the one whose 'cultural memory' stretched back to the early days.

In 1838, Justice Burton asked Cowper to report on the unsuccessful attempts at Aboriginal mission prior to the CMS Mission at Wellington Valley. This latest attempt was experiencing troubles, arising largely from protracted difficulties between the missionaries, which would eventually see the mission closed in 1842.

CHAPTER 3 | TWO ARCHDEACONS AND A BISHOP (1821–1842)

Cowper wrote his report on 11 June 1838. Although it took some weeks for news to reach Sydney, as it turned out this was two days after the cold-blooded murder of at least twenty-eight Aboriginal people on the Big (Gwydir) River in Northern NSW. By September, eleven men had been committed for trial, at about the same time an Aborigines' Protection Society came into existence in the colony, with William a committee member. By the end of the year, the 'Myall Creek Massacre' was being heatedly discussed as the culprits were tried on two occasions, resulting in seven of them being condemned to death for the crime. Three public petitions and jurors from both trials begged for mercy for the men, but they were still hung. This was a turning point in the relations between white and Aboriginal Australia.

Four of the men were Protestants, which meant it was William Cowper's duty to attend to them in the cells and at the gibbet. As many in Sydney had clamoured for the white men's release and harassed the jurymen of the second trial, Christian pulpits around the town had proclaimed that the equality and full humanity of the Aboriginal victims demanded appropriate punishment. Having recently reviewed the history of Aboriginal mission, in the awareness that one of the motives for mission was to try to prevent this kind of atrocity, Cowper must have had a mixture of feelings when he watched the men drop to the end of their rope.

Governor Gipps had stood firm during this troubled time for the colony. The indigenous population was equal before the law, and the heinous crime was one against humanity, and it must be punished. He also had to steer the colony towards the abolition of Transportation of convicts, and to grasp the nettle of General Education once again. Neither of these issues were uncontroversial, and his push towards General Education caused him to clash with his old school mate Bishop Broughton.

Massacre at Myall Creek – 1838[1]	
Early June	40 aboriginal people set up camp on Myall Creek Station
9 June	12 Stockmen arrive. They slaughter 28 aboriginal men, women and children
14–15 June	Overseer William Hobbs hears of the massacre and returns to the property
	Hobbs writes to Henry Dangar, property owner, has second thoughts and destroys letter.
	Hobbs relents, writes a second letter to Dangar and one to Police Magistrate Edward Denny Day
28 July	Day arrives under orders from Governor Gipps to bring the perpetrators to justice. Finds massacre site cleaned up
	Day arrests 11 men, one having escaped. Spends 47 days investigating
September	The eleven are committed to trial for the murder of aboriginal 'Daddy'
	Robert Scott, a wealthy magistrate, presided over a meeting to raise funds for the men's defence, and gives advice to the prisoners about the trial
15 November	Trial begins, under Justice Dowling. Robert Scott sits with the defence
	After deliberating for fifteen minutes, the jury finds the eleven not guilty to the excitement of the courtroom
	Immediately it is announced that the prisoners were remanded for trial for the murder of other Aboriginals
	Most of the Sydney press up in arms. Edward Hall, of the Monitor, expresses disgust at the jury's verdict and implies that others in high places were also guilty
27 November	Second trial begins before Justice Burton. Seven of the men convicted of murder
5 December	Three judges dismiss a demurrer, thus declaring the guilty verdict valid
7 December	Legislative Council deliberates and the Governor orders the men to be executed
	11 jurors from first trial and 10 from second petition the Governor for mercy. Three public petitions presented
	The seven confess, but say they didn't know killing blacks was a crime
18 December	The seven convicted murderers hanged. William Cowper attends the four Protestants

1. Adapted from Bill Wannan, *Early Australian Scandals*, ch.6.

At other times the Governor saw eye to eye with the Churchmen. In April 1839, when Gipps chaired a meeting of the Temperance Society, he was full of praise for the remarkable success this organisation had enjoyed world-wide in the short period of its existence. The local group, less than five years old, was 'engaged in fighting an uphill battle', 'as soldiers of the Cross fighting' for hearing God's word and keeping his commandments. Governing a colony in which nine tenths of the crime and misery could be traced to the use of ardent spirits, Gipps longed for the reverse of Jesus' famous miracle, that of turning ardent spirits into water. William Cowper, who in July would present a petition against distillation bearing 600 signatures to the Legislative Council, agreed with the Governor. Sydney's parish clergyman urged those who indulge in intoxication to attend a place of worship instead, and if this makes an impression on their minds, there would be no more need for gaols, or judges. For Cowper, it was being touched by the grace of God that led to social renovation.

Since 1837, NSW had been in the grip of a drought that would last until 1842 and cause the fall of land prices and the onset of a depression in 1841. In the midst of these difficult times, however, William and Harriette experienced the joy of another son born into this world, when, on 12 March 1839, Sedgwick Spelman Cowper joined them at the Parsonage.

Hard times were starting to bite, even in the city. In May 1839, the Committee of the Sydney Dispensary, heard that it had been a 'very sickly' year. In July, the Benevolent Society began a two month campaign soliciting special contributions in aid of 'the unprecedented large number and increasing cases' of those wanting to enter the Asylum. In August, a public meeting resulted in some action in response to the present needs, with the formation of 'The Sydney Association for the Temporary Relief of the Poor'. Charles spoke at the public meeting and William found himself on the Committee.

Although it was probably not an ideal time to be raising funds, on 30 December 1839, the parishioners of St Philip's met to discuss a much-awaited second church for the parish. William Cowper requested that it be called Holy Trinity, in order to give that doctrine a prominence. He also hoped that he might be spared to see further Schools opened in the parish. By this stage, Cowper was having increasing trouble with his eyesight.

Since Cowper lived to a great age, it is easy to overlook the fact that his years as Chaplain were studded with periods of severe illness, including eighteen attacks of ophthalmia. By the forties, the time had come when something had to be done. On 23 June 1840, William had the joy of laying the foundation stone for Holy Trinity. William's joy was tempered, however, since he was still grieving over the death of Harriette's second daughter, 9 day old Isabella, on 5 June. As he laid the stone, he also alluded to his own personal afflictions: his eyesight was failing rapidly. This had already caused him to resign

The subscription list for the Society for Temporary Relief of the Poor. The *Sydney Gazette* 7 Sept 1839.

The Macquarie Place Parsonage would be behind the viewer to the right.

Sydney Cove, ca 1830. Mrs Heriot Anley. State Library of NSW: ML 374.

from being secretary of the Diocesan Committee in March, and in August he also resigned from his responsibilities with the Benevolent Society, although agreeing to become Vice President. Far from his ill health diminishing his capacities, however, his congregation noticed a fervour in his preaching like they had never seen before.

In April 1841, the press announced Cowper's intention, because of cataracts in both eyes, to return to England—perhaps forever. On 10 September a public meeting opened a list for subscriptions towards defraying the costs of the voyage and the surgery. On 5 February, 1842, his portrait was published. On 18 February, after a church service led by his son, a large crowd presented their parson with an affectionate address and sufficient subscription money to pay all costs. After William gave an equally affectionate reply, more than 500 people walked him to the wharf.

As William, Harriette, Elizabeth and Sedgwick sailed on the *Hamlet*, Cowper carried a letter from Broughton to Edward Coleridge, in which the Bishop showed little hope of Cowper's recovery and return to useful duties in NSW. Behind this great show of affection, can be detected a suspicion that it was time to say a last goodbye to Sydney's first parish clergyman.

By 1842 the penal colony was well on its way towards becoming a free society. The extraordinary beginnings were moving towards the more ordinary life of a nation. William's ministry had also developed its own patterns, with an ordinary order and rhythm. But now, it seemed that the loss of his physical vision would prevent Cowper from pursuing his Christian vision any further.

4 | Evangelicalism Threatened and Defended (1843–1852) | Vision Stands Firm

*I*N THE FINAL PHASE of his ministry following his return to New South Wales, William Cowper increasingly found himself to be the champion of evangelical Protestantism. Cowper was a Protestant by conviction. But because he was an evangelical, his understanding of the Christian life and ministry differed from others in the Church of England, who nevertheless delighted in being Protestant. Protestantism was in his background, his history, the Church of his ordination. Evangelicalism was in his relational network, his reading matter, and in his own piety and pastoral practice. It was also deeply embedded in the laity of his parish. When his evangelical Protestantism came under threat, the normally amenable Cowper rose up in defence. For Cowper, this mattered immensely, for the gospel he had learned at the feet of the Reformers, and the view of life and ministry he had imbibed from the evangelical revival, brought the only real hope for those under his pastoral care.

The spire in the centre is St James'.

View from Darlinghurst, 1835. Frederick Garling. State Library of NSW: DL Pd 257.

The whole of Australia, it seemed, showed great interest in the progress of the Sydney parson's eye surgery. In March 1843, a rumour circulated at Port Phillip that two operations had failed, but this was almost immediately scotched by a more accurate report. He had endured three operations, and a fourth was likely, but the results were already promising. His sight was improving, he was now able to read large print with either eye, and his surgeon was confident he would return to Sydney with two good eyes.

St Philip's Church, Church Hill, St Patrick's Church, Fleury del., 1853. (Sydney: Sands & Kenny, 1855). National Library of Australia: nla.pic-an8434132.

Seal attached to William Cowper's Doctor of Divinity Testamur. Courtesy: Sydney Diocesan Archives. Photo: Peter Bolt.

Census of NSW, 2nd March 1841—from Pridden, *Australia* (1843).		
	NSW	Sydney
Population	130,856	29,973
Males	87,298	
Females	43,558	
Free	101,749	
Bondage	26,977	
Houses (mostly built of wood)	16,776	
Church of England	73,727	16,505
Presbyterian	13,153	3,111
Rome	35,690	8,126
Protestant Dissenters, including Wesleyans	5,093	1,707
Jews	856	462
Mahometans and Pagans	207	62

Before Cowper left England, William Howley, Archbishop of Canterbury, conferred upon him the Lambeth Palace Doctor of Divinity degree. This honour, recommended by Broughton, was awarded for his long service to the colony. Across the years to come, the colony would continue the honour by calling their pastor 'Dr Cowper'.

On Saturday, 5 August 1843, William, Harriette, and their two children, arrived home on the *Euphrates*. By Monday, the *Sydney Morning Herald* could report that 'that much esteemed gentleman has returned to the colony in excellent health, and that his sight is restored to him, so that he can read the smallest print'. Although he may have developed a strangely staring look, the Parish of Sydney welcomed their beloved clergyman back amongst them with his vision renewed.

Protestant Mr Cowper arrived to find a new Catholic Church being completed just below St Philip's on Church Hill—perhaps symbolic of the controversial times lying ahead of him. In England, after four decades of steps in this direction, the Catholic Relief Act of 1829 removed restrictions placed upon Roman Catholics in the Reformation period. In NSW, Governor Bourke, disliking the sectarianism of his native Ireland and convinced that the notion of an Established Church would not work in the colony, by the Church Act of July 1836, instituted a system in which government funds were given to the various denominations, in proportion to their numbers. In 1833 he had estimated one fifth of NSW were Roman Catholics. Since the arrival of John Bede Polding in 1835, the numbers of Catholic priests, schools and churches had been increasing.

While Cowper was away having his surgery, Bishop Broughton—no great supporter of Bourke's reforms in church or educational matters—had had his own clashes with Rome. Back as far as 1839, at a meeting presided over by Polding, the Catholics of Sydney had petitioned against a Protestant bishop having a seat on the Legislative

Council. His letters in this period show an increasing concern for the inroads being made by the Roman Catholics, and, for him, the rise of St Patrick's on Church Hill was definitely symbolic of his territory being invaded. But this came to a head for Broughton in March 1843, when Polding arrived back from a trip to Rome, under the title 'Archbishop of Sydney'. Two weeks later Bishop Broughton publicly and formally protested at this perceived imposition into his Episcopal territory. By 1851 he was still hurting that no-one had taken any notice.

But the threat was not just external. Almost as soon as the Roman Catholics received new recognition in England, Catholicism began to be emancipated within the ranks of the Church of England clergy. What was later called 'the Oxford Movement' (after its place of origin), 'Tractarianism' (after the associated series of *Tracts for the Times*), or 'Puseyism' (by its detractors, after one of its leaders), began with a sermon preached by John Keble in Oxford on 14 July 1833. This movement called for a rediscovery of the pre-Reformation catholic heritage of the Church of England. Perhaps inevitably therefore, in the mid forties a number of Church of England Clergy converted to Rome, which they regarded as having a greater claim to continuity with this period.

Many of the younger clergy coming to NSW came already influenced by this new movement. W. Macquarie later recalled that the impact of the Oxford teachings were 'a great grief' to his father. By the mid forties, Dr Cowper was vehemently opposed to the 'Puseyism' that seemed to be infecting Sydney, speaking out against it even at the Diocesan Committee in the presence of the Bishop.

Seat of the Revd W. Cowper D.D. Unknown artist. State Library of NSW: PXA 972/19.

Sectarian debates were now also part of NSW politics. While William was in England, Charles Cowper had become more involved in politics. In 1842, he had been active on the 'Petition Committee', which had been in existence since the early thirties, seeking the right for NSW to have a representative assembly. Once the right was granted, the elections of June 1843 were marred by violent riots in some counties, with people being stabbed and maimed—one man even dying from his wounds. Charles stood for nomination in Camden, but was defeated by Roger Therry. When Charles then stood for Cumberland, he was accused of creating religious division, because of some remarks made in the previous contest about Therry's Catholicism. Charles nevertheless won the election. The one who would later be known as 'slippery Charlie' had now embarked on the path in which he would earn a knighthood and serve NSW five times as Premier.

Premiers of NSW

1856 (June)	Sir Stuart Donaldson
1856 (August)	Sir Charles Cowper
1856 (October)	Sir Henry Parker
1857	Sir Charles Cowper
1859	William Forrester
1860	Sir John Robertson
1861	Sir Charles Cowper
1863	Sir James Martin
1865	Sir Charles Cowper
1866	Sir James Martin
1868	Sir John Robertson
1870	Sir Charles Cowper
1870 (December)	Sir James Martin
1877	Sir Henry Parkes

These years were not so full of triumph for Charles' other siblings. The long years of drought (since 1837), followed by the depression (since 1841), had taken its toll—and not only amongst those who depended on the land. Although continuing to practice medicine in Bungonia, between June 1842 and June 1844, Henry had fallen amongst the insolvent, and Thomas also joined that number from December 1843 to March 1844. Mary and George were also in difficulty, being forced to mortgage property in 1842–3, including 320 acres to father William for £1,000 (at 7%). George falling ill in 1846, and being forced to retire, compounded their

William Macquarie Cowper's Church and Parsonage.

Stroud Church, ca 1854. Conrad Martens (1801–1878). State Library of NSW: V*/Sp Coll/Martens/39.

financial problems, and they never really recovered. Mac was no doubt protected, since he was drawing a more secure salary as Chaplain to the Australian Agricultural Company at Stroud, where he had now been for six years. There must have been some interesting family discussions at this time, since in the church circles in which William, Charles and Mac moved, insolvency was spoken of as a moral failing.

Soon after Cowper's return, Governor Gipps had another attempt at introducing the system of General Education that had been defeated under Governor Bourke. The renewed controversy must have made Cowper wonder if he had been away! In August 1844, St Philip's Parochial Association stated its firm opposition to the scheme of education being considered by the Legislative Council. After hearing an address from Cowper on the principles of education, the meeting endorsed these principles, which had always been enshrined in the education given at the St Philip's schools. It then expressed its opposition to the Government's proposed scheme, believing 'the doctrines of Divine Revelation to constitute an essential part of a sound education, and that the *well-being of the State* cannot be secured without giving religious instruction to the children'. By September, the issue was flaring hot. On Monday 2 September, while the Catholic supporters of Rev. John McEnroe's system stormed a meeting of the Friends of General Education, members of the Church of England had been summoned by their city clergy to discuss an education based on the principles of their own Church. Bishop Broughton addressed them at length, and his speech was published in the press along with

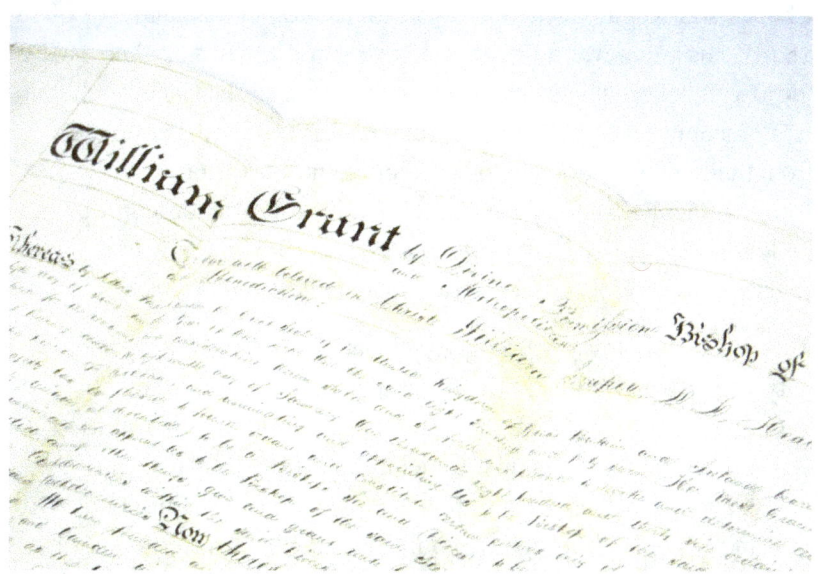

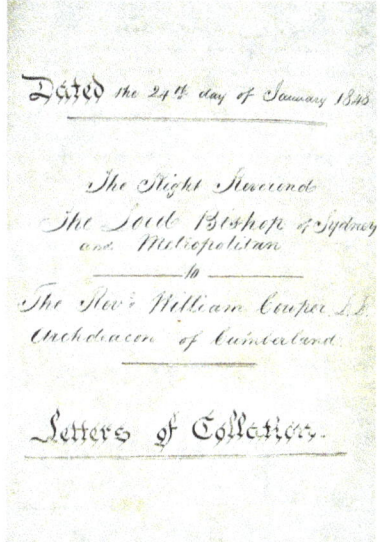

Letters of Collation of William Cowper, 24 January 1848. Courtesy: Sydney Diocesan Archives. Photo: Peter Bolt.

many other pages devoted to the issue. Once again, the government could not gain a complete victory, although this time it met with some success. By January 1848, two boards of education had been established, one General, and one Denominational.

January 1848 also brought further regularisation of the Church, along with new responsibilities for the St Philip's parson. Bishop Broughton, drawing upon the authority vested in him by his Letters Patent, constituted the Counties of Camden and Cumberland into the Archdeaconry of Cumberland, and appointed Cowper its first Archdeacon. At the same time further Letters Patent of 25 June 1847 were read, dividing the Bishoprick of Australia into four distinct Dioceses. Bishops Short, for Adelaide, Perry, for Melbourne, and Tyrrell, for Newcastle had already arrived. This meant further changes locally, and on 26 January, Cowper, in one of his earliest duties as Archdeacon, led Bishop Broughton by the hand to the seat within the communion rails at St Andrew's Church, and installed and inducted him as the Bishop of Sydney.

Bishop Tyrrell was present for Broughton's Wednesday installation, before taking the steamer to Newcastle on Saturday. On Sunday, he attended Christ Church where he heard G.K. Rusden preach in the morning and W. Macquarie Cowper in the evening. The son of the new Archdeacon of Cumberland also had the responsibility for reading the prayers for Tyrrell's installation the next day. With almost a dozen years already served in what had now become the Newcastle

A caricature of Dean William Macquarie Cowper, at a much later date.

An ecclesiastical relic, Dean Cowper, 20 Oct 1888. Phil May (1864–1903). State Library of NSW: SV/134.

CHAPTER 4 | EVANGELICALISM THREATENED AND DEFENDED (1843–1852)

Diocese, and another eight to go, Macquarie Cowper soon became one of Tyrrell's closest companions, as the 'bachelor bishop' commenced building this new Diocese.

It did not take long for the newly ordered Sydney Diocese to be struck with controversy. In February 1848, two clergymen, Robert Knox Sconce and Thomas Makinson, under the influence of the new Oxford teaching, defected to Rome. Sconce had previously confided his position to Charles Cowper, with full awareness that he could not stay within the Church of England holding the views that he had come to. Charles was sanguine when he wrote to his brother Macquarie (23 Feb 1848): 'His going will do good to a great many. It will stop their saying "don't you believe it", "there is no danger", "it is all the Geneva school"'. It is probably a sign of Sydney's strong evangelical laity that nobody from their congregations followed Sconce and Makinson Rome-ward. No other clergyman took this step either. Instead, Archdeacon Cowper and nineteen Sydney clergy, presented Bishop Broughton with a statement of condolence at the two secessions.

This was a real blow for Broughton's relationship with the Sydney laity, in particular. Already there was a great deal of discontent about his newer clergy with Tractarian tendencies. In 1844, during Broughton's campaign against General Education, the Speaker of the Legislative Council asked him how people could trust Church of England Schools, if Broughton couldn't guarantee his clergy. Because of the need for clergy, Broughton had supported the foundation of St Augustine's College in Canterbury, which English evangelicals soon opposed as 'Puseyite'. When Cowper took up this cry locally, Broughton found almost no-one would give a subscription to it. He had opened his own St James' College in 1845, but it, too, had been

(Old) St Philip's Church. Unknown Artist. State Library of NSW: PXA 972/12.

rumoured to encourage Tractarian doctrines, and Sconce himself had taught there. By 1849, it was forced to close its doors. When Broughton refused to ordain two deacons, Beamish and Russell, after they spoke against the presence of Tractarianism at St James' College and in the Diocese, the gap between bishop and laity opened even further.

Happier times came for Cowper in mid year, when on 1 May 1848, the foundation stone was laid for the new St Philip's. William had become used to talking of the 'old church', and adding to his annual Returns to the Government a note about the need to accommodate more people. The moment had finally come for a new building, which symbolised for him a further step forward in the work of the gospel in the parish of Sydney.

The laying of the stone was also an occasion when Sydney's long-serving clergyman was unexpectedly honoured. Cowper was so moved by the occasion that he had difficulty at times conducting the preceding Church service. With the prayers said, the congregation walked up to the peak of the hill to the site of the new Church. Just at the required moment, Broughton handed the St Philip's parson the trowel, saying:

Portrait of the Venerable Archdeacon Cowper, D.D., 1854. Walter G. Mason, after Claxton. National Library of Australia: nla.pic-an7978970.

> It does appear to me that the long years of your connection with this parish as its minister, and the intimate and affectionate relationship subsisting between yourself and the parishioners entitle you to the honour of laying this foundation stone. Allow me, therefore, to request that you will have the goodness to perform that duty which under other circumstances I should have had much pleasure in performing.[1]

Dr Cowper expressed his deep sense of honour at this duty. He laid the stone with the usual formula for such occasions: 'as the foundation of a church in that parish for the preaching of the right Catholic Faith, which we believe and confess, in the name of the Father, the Son, and the Holy Ghost'.[2] But, mindful of the recent controversies, this formula took on additional meaning. This was a statement affirming the direction the ministry at St Philip's would continue to take. Despite the claims of the Tractarians, Cowper's evangelical Protestantism was the *right* Catholic Faith.

Tragedy struck the family the next year, when, on 5 June 1849, Henry Cowper died, aged just 48, leaving Eliza struggling financially. At the time, William himself was so severely ill, that he felt he had come to his own end. When he emerged from 'the valley of the shadow of death', he preached a sermon that provides a glimpse into why he held his

1. W.M. Cowper, *Autobiography & Reminiscences*, 55.
2. W.M. Cowper, *Autobiography & Reminiscences*, 56.

St Phillips Church, 1848. Joseph Fowles (1810–1878). From *Sydney in 1848*.

Evangelical Protestant convictions so firmly.

Resuming the pulpit on 14 October 1849, William selected as his text Psalm 141:7: 'Our bones lie scattered at the grave's mouth'. In view of the severity of his illness, he explained that he stood before the congregation 'as a monument of [God's] mercy, love, and power'. He spoke of how, even at death's door, his soul was untroubled, because he trusted 'in the all sufficient atonement of Jesus Christ'.

In contrast to this sure ground of evangelical assurance, he then spoke strongly against Tractarian doctrines and practices:

> Not all the infidelity, nor all the neology, now so prevalent and fashionable in almost every civilized community, not all the unscriptural doctrines, or devices of Popery or Puseyism, not any saints, or ceremonies, not any supposed sacramental efficacy, not any mere Baptismal regeneration, without the renewing of the Holy Ghost, not any presumed merit of the Lord's Supper, could afford peace to the conscience; ... [3]

After thirty-nine years of ministry in this harsh land, having buried so many that he had baptised and married, and having stood at the gibbet as hundreds of prisoners took their final journey, the pastor was well aware of his people's greatest enemy.

A later picture of Charles, as Premier of New South Wales.

Charles Cowper, Premier. J. Roarty. State Library of NSW: PXA 549/ 24c.

Death is inevitable, he went on, and the tragedies of human life are a reminder of the duty of preparing for another world. These words recall that his own life had had its fair share of tears. He had lost two wives, and seen the impact on his motherless children. He had now also lost two children, as well as several grandchildren. It was no mere theological theory to him when he pleaded with the congregation:

> Cannot he, who was a husband, or she, who was a wife, yet remember the day when God was pleased to take away the partner, endeared by many strong proofs of conjugal affection? Cannot the parent also remember the time when the Lord gave, and when the Lord took away the beloved child? Cannot the child likewise remember when God removed the kind and watchful parent, that best earthly friend and protector? [...] By all these, and innumerable other instances of daily mortality, does not our God teach us plainly, that in like manner, he will also visit us, and take us away?[4]

Puseyism brought no assurance at this hour of greatest need.

---

3. W. Cowper, *A Sermon*, 3–4.
4. W. Cowper, *A Sermon*, 9.

Cowper's own confidence was the 'all sufficient atonement of Christ', as proclaimed by his evangelical Protestantism. He therefore closed his message with passionate exhortations to be ready, by clinging to Jesus Christ, who brings the victory over death and so provides triumphant assurance at 'the departing hour'.[5]

With Henry gone, Thomas was now the eldest of the children. On January 28, 1850, he left for California on the *Orator*, probably in search of better fortune. While he was in San Francisco, he had a portrait done of himself. But Thomas was once again disappointed. A letter home speaks of a failed attempt to sell some horses in Panama, and the need to purchase his ticket home by writing a bill against his father. Hoping William would pay for his passage, Thomas arrived home on 29 April 1851 aboard the *Mercury*.

Portrait of Thomas Cowper, ca. 1850–51. Unknown artist. Warren Kenny Family Archive.

Charles had become the Manager of the Australian Railway Company. On 3rd July, 1850, about 10,000 people turned out in the pouring rain, to watch the daughter of Colonel Stewart (Lt. Governor, 1825) turn the sod for Australia's first railway. After wheeling turf away in a barrow, Charles then addressed the crowd, telling them how gratified he was to reach this moment after four and a half years of working towards it. 'As regards the moral and social advancement of the colony', Charles had difficulty in finding another event to compare it with.

Turning of the turf of the first Australian Railway, Sydney, 3 July 1850, 1893. John Rae (1813–1900). National Library of Australia: nla.pic-an10759912-S27.

For the entire month of October 1850, the six Bishops of Australasia gathered together in their first conference. Halfway through, they were presented with an address, over numerous signatures, read by Archdeacon Cowper, to which Bishop Broughton responded. Their agenda included education and mission to the aboriginals of the islands of the Western Pacific and of Australia. But their primary concern was how the colonial church should be governed, once the Church of England had moved away from a homeland in which it was part of the establishment. The Bishops' proposals for a structure of government that gave a real place for both clergy and laity set a lead for Anglicans elsewhere in the world.

5. W. Cowper, *A Sermon*, 11.

But one outcome of the Bishop's conference did not please the local evangelical clergy and laity of Sydney. In November, no doubt Cowper was amused to find wax models in excellent likeness of himself on display at the Australasian Botanic and Horticultural Society's summer exhibition. But, at the time, he was probably much more concerned that all of the bishops, with the exception of the evangelical Perry, had endorsed the doctrine of baptismal regeneration. This was a bitter disappointment to evangelical laity all over Australia, but especially in Sydney.

The laity's already festering discontent with Broughton just got worse. His Tractarian clergy, his 'Puseyite' Colleges, and now the other Bishops —that, in effect, he had invited in—had avowed a doctrine that was clearly more Catholic than Evangelical. As the gap widened between the Bishop and the people in the pews, Archdeacon Cowper increasingly found himself in the middle, as something of a bridge between bishop and layman. By default, he had become the evangelical statesman of the Diocese of Sydney.

The Government escort and mail containing the gold, arrival at the treasury, Sydney, 1851. Marshall Claxton (1811–1881). National Library of Australia: nla.pic-an6629355-1.

In 1851, as the good and ill effects of the discovery of gold began to be felt in church and society, Broughton waited for a response from the Archbishop of Canterbury in regard to the right of the Australian Church to govern itself. Broughton also took the opportunity to remind Canterbury, once again, about his 1843 protest, which had apparently fallen on deaf ears. When the response arrived, it was unsatisfactory, ignoring the question of the government of the Australian Church. Broughton called a meeting of his clergy in April

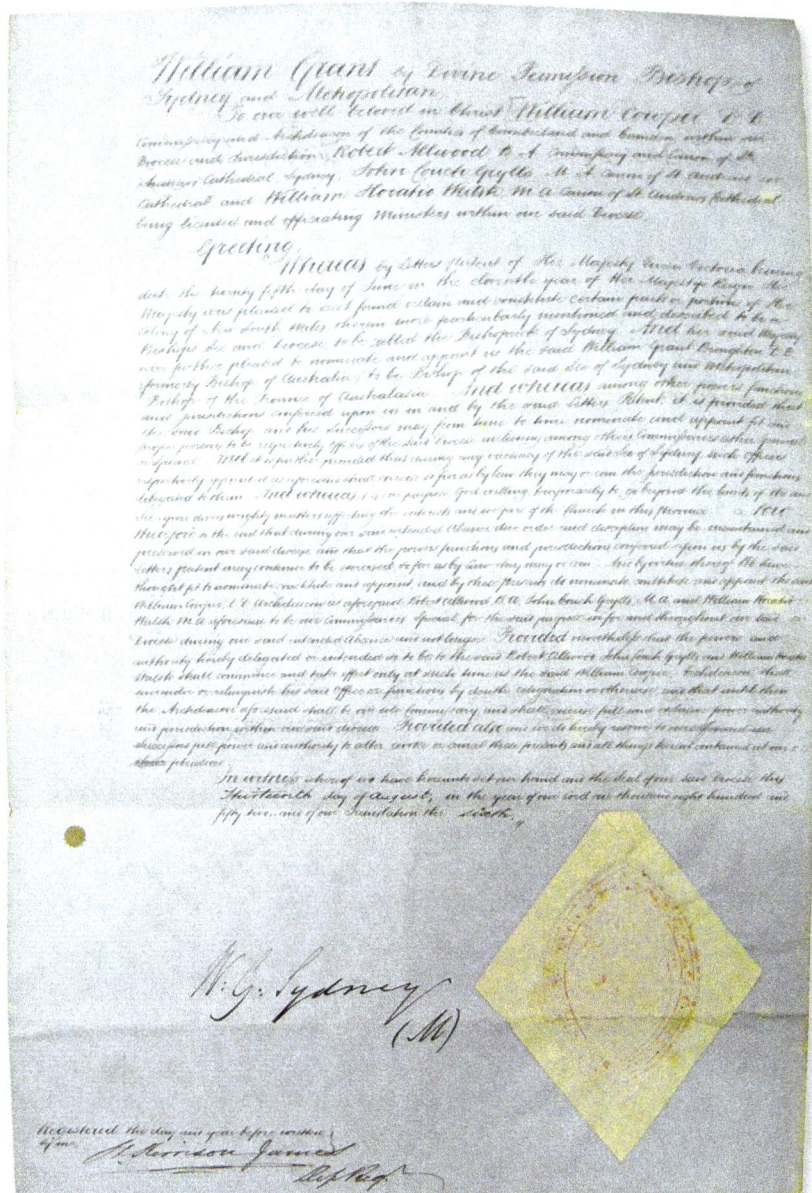

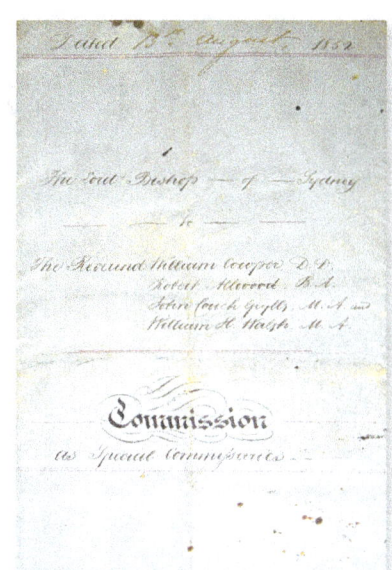

Appointment of W. Cowper as Bishop Broughton's sole Commissary. Courtesy: Sydney Diocesan Archives. Photo: Peter Bolt.

1852 to draw up a petition to the Queen, praying for power to be given to frame a constitution. In order to present the petition personally, and consult more widely about these matters, he planned a voyage to England.

On Friday the 13th, August 1852, Broughton appointed Archdeacon Cowper as his 'sole Commissary', with the right to 'exercise full and extensive power, authority and jurisdiction' within the Diocese, during the Bishop's absence. After being farewelled by his clergy with an affectionate address on Saturday, and by the Diocese at the Cathedral on Sunday, Broughton embarked and sailed for England. He would never return.

Cowper, now almost 74 years old, found himself in charge of Sydney Diocese. His Evangelical Protestant vision appeared to be under attack from influential quarters. And yet he was all the more convinced that it needed to be upheld. People were looking to him for evangelical leadership, but what could he do? As Commissary, he was to serve in the Bishop's footsteps. Little did he know, that this would be for longer than first expected.

CHAPTER 4 | EVANGELICALISM THREATENED AND DEFENDED (1843–1852)

5 | Responsibility to Reward
(1852-1858) | Vision Bequeaths a Future

*D*OING HIS DUTY HAD always been part of Cowper's piety, and he willingly grasped his ministerial labours with both hands. But being made sole Commissary of the Diocese of Sydney at this time in the Colony's history, and in the latter stages of his life, proved a great strain on him. The need for ministry was still rapidly expanding. The general population was unsettled due to the discovery of gold. The early fifties were a time of bitter factionalism in the Diocese, in the aftermath of Tractarian/Evangelical controversies in England and their counterpart in Australia. And then there was, in Sydney, the rift that had opened up between the laity and at least some of the clergy, which continued to need some healing. Across the last decade, Cowper had emerged as a spokesman of evangelicalism and a friend of the laity, and now he was left in charge.

After decades of battling for education in the schools to be along Church of England Principles, the battle had recently entered the tertiary sphere. Before Broughton left, he bitterly opposed the plans to establish the University of Sydney along General Education lines, with Cowper in support. With Broughton gone, Bishop Tyrrell had taken up the charge, again, ably supported by William Cowper in Sydney—and William Macquarie Cowper in Newcastle. When some of the Clergy were amongst the 700 strong crowd at the inauguration of the University on 11 October 1852, Bishop and Archdeacon were agreed

BELOW LEFT: Later engraving of Charles. *The Hon. Charles Cowper, delegate from New South Wales, 1863.* State Library of Victoria: IMP04/04/63/8 (b48668).

BELOW RIGHT: The famous later portrait of William Macquarie, as the ancient Dean of Sydney.
Portrait of William Macquarie Cowper, Dean of Sydney (188–?). John Hubert Newman, 1830–1916. National Library of Australia. NLA: PIC PIC/7655 LOC Box PIC/7655. nla.pic-an24084521.

THE HON. CHARLES COWPER,

that this had weakened their stand, and Tyrrell took a trip to Sydney to attempt to regain ground in the battle. Both men penned letters to the newspapers condemning the absence of Divinity teaching at the new University. Charles was also involved on the political side.

The dream of Australia's first tertiary college went back at least as far as Archdeacon Scott's days. His plans came to expression in 1830, when the Corporation of Clergy and School Lands proposed the establishment of two King's Schools, as feeders for the higher College. In these plans, of course, it was simply assumed that the education at every level would be according to the Principles of the United Church of England and Ireland. In the minds of Archdeacons Scott and Broughton, this would be a means by which the clergy of the colony would be supplied. As Bishop, Broughton kept the dream alive, and in 1840 when Thomas Moore left his huge fortune to the Church of England for exactly this purpose, it looked like Liverpool would become the seat of Australia's first tertiary college, and therefore, at last be put on the map.

Portrait of William Macquarie Cowper. Australian Town & Country Journal, 22 January 1876, p.133. State Library of NSW: TN83.

But in the Colony of New South Wales, the Church of England could no longer be regarded as the Established Church. The previous long struggle for an appropriate form of education in such a colony had sharpened the issues for tertiary education as well. The mistrust of Broughton and his clergy by Sydney's laity had also added to the volatile mixture. The University of Sydney was to be an institution that favoured no particular creed and any 'Church Principles' were to be taught in the affiliated Colleges. Broughton, Tyrrell and Cowper were still not happy with the compromise.

In late May 1853, the news reached NSW that Bishop Broughton had died on 20 February. On his voyage home, yellow fever had broken out on the vessel, carrying off ten of the crew, including the Captain. Broughton reached Southampton already feeble. After recovering he visited his elderly mother, spoke at meetings of the SPG and SPCK and preached in London. He was suddenly seized with an attack of Bronchitis, and he died shortly afterwards.

St Phillip's (now taken down), Church Hill, N.S.W., 1852. By 'T.T.' National Library of Australia: nla.pic-an5370122.

CHAPTER 5 | RESPONSIBILITY TO REWARD (1852–1858)

The sad news came to Cowper at a time of great joy. The same week, he had heard the report that his new Church was progressing well, a healthy amount of money had been subscribed, and the stonework would be completed before Christmas. When this joy was interrupted by the news of the Broughton's death, the Archdeacon convened a meeting on 31 May for a testimonial in honour of his late Bishop. Cowper added his own speech to the high praise of Broughton's energy, virtues, and piety. As a fitting memorial, the meeting resolved to establish the Broughton Scholarship at the King's School.

St Paul's College, Sydney, 1856.
Samuel Thomas Gill (1818–1880).
National Library of Australia: nla.pic-an7537510.

Ironically, it was probably the death of the Bishop of Sydney that enabled a compromise to be reached in regard to the University Colleges. On 29 July, Cowper chaired a meeting at which the Bishops of Newcastle and New Zealand were present. The meeting heard how Bishop Selwyn had urged the importance of churchmen uniting together and how a package of measures had been agreed upon. The University had agreed to require from each graduate a certificate of competency in religious attainments from their college. The meeting then passed a series of resolutions unanimously, with the only objection being over the name of the college. It was changed from Queen's College to Trinity College, although, by November, it had become 'St Paul's'. The same meeting also resolved that the Governor be requested to grant the Old Burial Ground in George Street, next to St Andrew's Cathedral, to the Church of England, so that a theological college might be constructed on the site. The need for clergy was still pressing, and, with the recent controversies, there was an increasingly strong opinion in Sydney that they needed to be trained locally.

Within weeks of Broughton's death, rumours about Broughton's successor had begun. Some spoke of Bishop Selwyn of New Zealand, but, in August, William wrote to Elizabeth, at Stroud, with the speculation that Bishop Tyrrell might take the position. If so, he asked, 'what will William do, if his good Bp should be translated? Will William come to Sydney?' But the appointment would be long delayed, and Cowper had to endure as sole Commissary until Bishop Barker arrived in May 1855.

On 6 December 1853, Cowper chaired a meeting of the Australian Board of Missions, which heard the report of a sub-committee appointed in March 1851 to enquire into the best means of instituting a successful mission to 'the aborigines of the colony'. The committee spoke of 'a lamentable falling off in the numbers of aborigines in the settled districts'. It recommended clergymen be sent to remote areas. More controversially (as time would tell), it urged that children should be separated from the adults, for the purpose of them 'being brought up in the ways of civilised life'.

The new year brought further acclaim, sadness, and controversy for Archdeacon Cowper. The acclaim began in January, 1854, when the *Illustrated Sydney News* printed an engraving (by W.G. Mason) after a new portrait of him by Marshall Claxton, accompanied by a brief biography in praise of almost 45 years of ministry. In March Cowper was honoured further, with a testimonial dinner at St Philip's Grammar School, during which Claxton's portrait was presented to him, in the hope that it would be 'handed down to posterity, and be preserved by your children in memory of your many virtues'. When Cowper replied with gratitude for their kindness, he added some pastoral admonitions. His continued concern about the Diocese came through, in his not-so-veiled allusions to Tractarianism, when he warned against some practices more recently introduced which threaten 'to prevent the pure gospel of Christ'.

Portrait of the Venerable Archdeacon Cowper, D.D., Walter G. Mason. *The Illustrated Sydney News*, 28 Jan 1854. Photo: Peter Bolt.

The sadness began in May, when George Brooks, daughter Mary's husband, eventually gave in to an eight-year illness, and died. His illness and subsequent retirement meant that the family had never really recovered from their financial difficulties, which Mary continued to carry until her own death on 17 April 1859. More sadness came on 21 October, when Mac's wife Margaret, aged 48, also passed away. She was buried between the church and the parsonage at Stroud next to her infant daughter Elizabeth Jane who had died in 1838. The inscriptions for both record a bold hope of the resurrection to come.

The controversy had been brewing for William since the beginning of the year, but it boiled over in May, when Justice Stephen published some correspondence in the *Herald*, concerning the treatment received by the Rev. John Milner. Milner had arrived in the Colony as a Naval Chaplain, but after he had been left behind due to illness, he assisted the ministry at Christ Church St Lawrence, Justice Stephen's congregation. Before Broughton had left, he had refused to license Milner due to a charge of some impropriety, which was then withdrawn. Despite this, however, Broughton still refused a licence, and Cowper, as Commissary, upheld this decision. Eventually Milner left the Colony, but Justice Stephen felt the matter should go public. When the correspondence was published, this rare glimpse of 'Cowper the controversialist' displayed the Archdeacon as firm in his convictions, but nevertheless able to deal with his opponents with a gentleness and grace.

The dining room at Wivenhoe.
Photo: Corinne Cowper.

In January 1855, William wrote to Elizabeth, at Wivenhoe, confessing that he was now working seven days a week, but nevertheless glad because it is work given to him by God. About the same time, he wrote to Sedgy, who had asked whether he could make the journey to Chatsbury, Charles' property north of Goulburn. William advised him to come home as early as he could, since he may have to return to W. Macquarie for lessons. Just as William once educated his older children at home, now one of those sons apparently educated half-siblings Elizabeth and Sedgwick (as well as nephew Charles) at his home in Stroud.

Elizabeth Ann Cowper.
Keith Cowper Family Archive.

By the time Barker arrived on 25 May, the Archdeacon was well and truly ready to hand things back to him. He was overjoyed to meet his new Bishop, greeting him as the answer to his prayers. As Bishop Frederic and his wife Jane stepped ashore, Cowper and many of the clergy and laity of Sydney welcomed them, before taking them to meet the Governor. In the afternoon, they held a service of thanksgiving at St Andrew's and Cowper read the Bishop an address of welcome. On the 30th, Archdeacon Cowper assisted in the installation of the new Bishop into his See. Cowper's joy and thankfulness was evident to all. He had prayed for a godly bishop, and one who would support and strengthen the evangelical Protestantism that once characterised the diocese, but had recently been under such threat. Barker wasted no time in getting to work, and, aware of the strain under which the elderly Archdeacon had been operating, he immediately relieved him of his Commissary's duties, so that he could concentrate on his parish —especially the completion of the new Church.

The strain of these years was certainly taking its toll on William. When the Barkers arrived, Jane noted certain things she found odd about him, attributing them to his age and implying that he was a little past it. Thomas Hassall later turned up to preach at St Philip's to find that William had forgotten he was coming. His health had previously caused him to worry about his own future and that of his family, and this time, on 5 January 1856, it caused him to make his Will, which provided especially for Harriette, and his two youngest children's education.

Portrait of Harriette Swaine, [after 1860]. Photo: E. Steele, Wisbech. Keith Cowper Family Archive.

Even before Barker came to Australia, he knew about the bequest of Thomas Moore towards a tertiary college. Three weeks after he arrived, he met with the other Trustees of Moore's Estate to announce his plans to open a training college for clergy in at Liverpool. In Stroud, William Macquarie was still grieving Margaret's loss, and his Bishop, although kindly, couldn't offer the comfort he needed, and his thoughts began to turn towards Sydney. Bishop Tyrrell, who also had thoughts of a college, had offered him the job of training the clergy for Newcastle, but it was Barker's invitation to become Acting Principal at Moore College that proved the most tempting. And so, on Saturday 1st March 1856, Moore College opened its doors at Liverpool, in Thomas Moore's old residence, with three students whom Mac had brought from amongst his pupils at Stroud.

Moore College, Liverpool, and Thomas Moore's House, [ca. 1865]. Courtesy: Moore College.

March must have been an exciting month for father William. Not only did Mac return 'home' and an evangelical training college begin, but, on 27 March 1856, the new St Philip's was consecrated. On the morning of Sunday 30th, William preached the first sermon in the

CHAPTER 5 | RESPONSIBILITY TO REWARD (1852–1858)

(New) St Philip's Church, Sydney, [1850–1859]. Walter G. Mason. National Library of Australia: nla.pic-an8329654.

new building, and his son preached the first evening sermon. William's sermon, 'The Benefits of Attending Public Worship', stressed the advantages the new building gave to the congregation, for worship and outreach. He concluded his exhortation with the hope that the new St Philip's would remind them all that they have 'a building of God, a house not made with hands, eternal in the heavens'.

This heavenly perspective which had characterised William's life and ministry, now came to dominate his last days. The fact that his own eternity loomed large caused him to reflect further upon that theme for his congregation. As his health declined, he used his convalescence for further literary productivity. He had begun reading in some new views on biblical prophecy, and this led to a series of three tracts: *Thoughts on the Resurrection of the Dead* (1856), *Thoughts on the New Creation* (1856), *and Thoughts on the Ages to Come* (1857). The subtitle of each tract, *'with reference to the Millennium'*, hints at the fact that Cowper's tracts each unfold an aspect of what we now know as Dispensationalism.

William Cowper to John Cowper, 29 Dec 1856. Stuart Calder Family Archive.

When a Warden for St Paul's College was appointed in November, Cowper resigned from acting in that position. With his last educational duty behind him, it is fair to say that he had been active in establishing in the Colony educational institutions from infants to tertiary levels. To him, education—and not just education, but especially education in the Scriptures—was a key strategy for ensuring the 'rising generation' would be a resource for the continued improvement of society.

With two tracts written already, on 28 December, 1856, he celebrated his 78th Birthday. The next day, he wrote to his elder brother John, enclosing the tracts for his attention. He recalled that 'nearly 70 years ago' John brought him back a tract from the Hawes' fair, a 'grave sermon' on Micah 2:10. It still left a clear impression on the old man, who now appealed to his older brother to trust in Jesus Christ, if he did not do so already.

By March, 1857, as Sydney added to its amenities with a new sewer, part of the improvements to cope with an expanding population, Cowper had become dangerously ill, so much so, that rumours circulated that he had died. He recovered, however, and when the Old St Philip's building was sold in July, he presented the pulpit, reading-desk, and sounding-board to the Bishop. In August, he must have been delighted to hear Barker turn to a subject dear to his own heart. Preaching in the St Philip's school-room, the Bishop urged a new enthusiasm for mission to the Aborigines, and expressed the hope that the indigenous people of Australia would have their own church established within thirty years.

Making the new sewer in Pitt Street, Sydney, 1857. Walter G. Mason. National Library of Australia: nla.pic-an8021132.

CHAPTER 5 | RESPONSIBILITY TO REWARD (1852–1858)

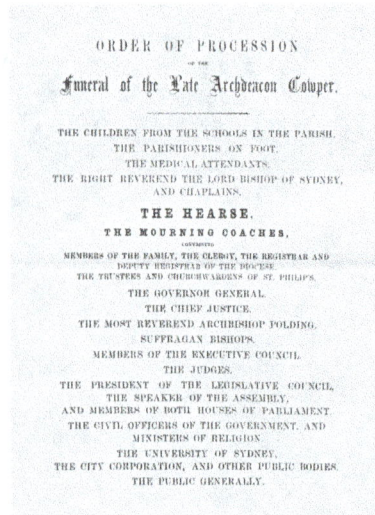

Order of Procession for the funeral of William Cowper, 9 July 1858. Keith Cowper Family Archive.

Sedgwick Spelman Cowper. Keith Cowper Family Archive.

Residence of Archdeacon Cowper, 1860. Frederick Charles Terry, 1826–1869. National Library of Australia: nla.pic-an5370153.

There were many other hopeful signs of improvement in the churches as 1858 opened, and the new Bishop's energy seemed boundless. In May, however, Cowper was suddenly seized with another severe bout of illness. By July, the press reported that 'his naturally strong frame has been struggling against the disease' but he was not responding to treatment. He was in no pain, and his intellect was 'perfectly unclouded'. Bishop Barker had been out of town, but when he arrived home, he went straight to the parsonage. Glad to see him, Cowper informed the Bishop, "I am waiting, at peace within, my summons to depart".

On the morning of 6 July, William received that summons, and, after forty-nine years as Sydney's parish clergyman, he at last entered his rest. In a special Government Gazette, Governor-General Denison announced his death and invited all Government officers to attend the funeral.

When that day came, on 9 July, the entire city stopped to say goodbye to their pastor. The procession moved slowly to the church and afterwards to the Devonshire Street Cemetery, hindered by the crowds at every point. The crowds gathered at the parsonage, hours before the appointed hour. The front of the long funeral procession arrived at St Philip's, Church Hill, before the other end had left the parsonage. When the procession arrived, the church was already full and there was hardly enough room for the coffin and the mourners to enter from the western door. It was the same again afterwards. As the procession moved slowly through the city to the Devonshire Street Cemetery, all the businesses had completely closed to allow people to line the streets. And line the streets they did. In 1858, there were 300,000 people in NSW, and 64,000 in Sydney, and yet an estimated 25,000 people thronged the streets of Sydney to watch Cowper's last earthly journey. This was the biggest funeral Sydney had ever seen.

When the official procession arrived at the cemetery, it was already so crowded that only those closest to William could even get near the graveside to hear Barker pronounce the final farewell, and the triumphant note that Cowper's body had been placed in the ground in the sure and certain hope of the resurrection from the dead.

Thomas was not in Sydney when his father died. He was a little surprised that the letter that found him up north on the Clarence River was not from Charles or William, but from the youngest of the family— now studying at Sydney University, but still affectionately known as 'Sedgy'. Thomas reassured his step-brother that their father's death need not be the end of their relationship, although he will probably have little cause to see him ever again. Contrary to some public reports that William had not been in pain, through Sedgy's 19 year old eyes his father had suffered greatly during his illness. Thomas is grieved that he did not receive the news of his father's last days until well after he was buried. Thomas comforted the young Sedgwick with the hope he evidently shared with his father:

*Portrait of the Ven. William Cowper, D.D.,
1854. Marshall Claxton (1811–1881).
Courtesy: Warden & Fellows, St Paul's
College University of Sydney.
Photo: Alice Bolt.*

> Much as we might have wished him to continue with us, it would have been wrong when so much happiness was awaiting him […] He is now released from all suffering and enjoying the actual presence of his Redeemer whom he served so long and so faithfully. I wish we may meet him.[1]

William Cowper, after a long and faithful ministry to both his physical and spiritual family, had at last received his reward.

On the following Sunday, funeral discourses were preached at St Philip's. After being awestruck with how many had lined the streets to say goodbye to the Sydney Parish Clergyman, Bishop Barker's sermon was clear about what had happened:

> It is universally acknowledged, that not only the Church to which he belonged, but the land in which he lived, has lost one of its brightest ornaments and the most revered of its sons.[2]

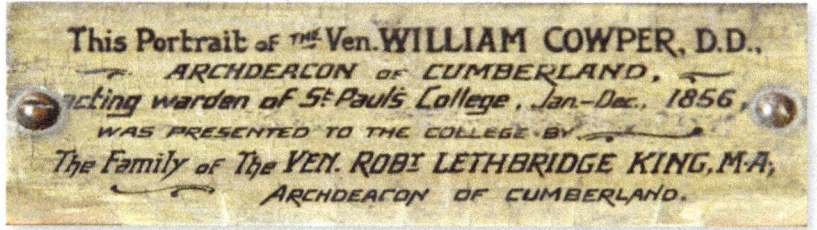

1. Thomas Cowper to Sedgwick Cowper, 28 July 1858 (Keith Cowper Family Archive).
2. Barker, *The Victor's Crown*, 14.

CHAPTER 5 | RESPONSIBILITY TO REWARD (1852–1858)

But, said the Bishop, if his life becomes an example for others, then he will not be lost. His memory would be embodied as others continued to live by the same vision.

In August 1809, William Cowper was hardly noticed when he arrived on the *Indispensable*. In July 1858, the city closed down while 25,000 people pressed around his funeral procession—a testimony to the deep impact the St Philip's clergyman had made on his parish and beyond.

From the beginning, Cowper faithfully and persistently gave himself to the work of Christian ministry. He brought the evangelical patterns he learned in Yorkshire to NSW. He preached, he prayed, he led Divine Worship, he lectured, he educated, he faithfully visited all classes of people to bring them the consolation found in the Lord Jesus Christ. His evangelical vision brought him to a disorderly penal colony, and worked him hard to build an orderly society in its place. His evangelical vision brought an assurance that was so essential for pastoral ministry in a context afflicted by the brevity and brutishness of life, that when he perceived it to be under attack, Cowper rose up in defence. As Australia's first parish clergyman, he etched these patterns of ministry deeply onto the landscape into which others later came.

St Philip's, Sydney, 2009. Photo: Peter Bolt.

It was his evangelical vision that also brought his children to NSW. They were part of that second generation, those who called Australia home. They each experienced their own joys, trials and sorrows. Through their pioneering efforts in medicine, farming and grazing, politics, Christian ministry, and engagement in social issues, they each in their own way left a legacy. And behind that legacy, stands the man who addressed them as their 'affectionate father, William Cowper'.

For Cowper, the clergyman's duties were essential for the building of society and ordering it for good. But the ordering of society in this present life was always with a view to the heavenly life to come, which never seemed to fade from Cowper's vision. The best thing that Cowper could do for his new land was to faithfully and persistently give himself to his clerical duties, preparing people to meet their God in the life to come. So that is what he did—day in, day out—for forty-nine years. That was the secret to his great influence.

On the day of his funeral Sydney stopped and one third of Sydney turned out to say goodbye to William Cowper—the indispensable parson.

Picture and Manuscript Acknowledgements

Cover   *Rev'd Dr William Cowper, senior chaplain of New South Wales*. Unknown artist. Richard Jones' album. Pencil Portrait. State Library of New South Wales: PXA 972/4.

(Old) St Philip's Church, Richard Jones' album. Unknown Artist. State Library of New South Wales: PXA 972/12.

Inside Cover   *Cowper Book Plate*. From *The First Report of the Auxiliary Bible Society of NSW* (1817): Courtesy: NSW Bible Society. Photo: John Cowper.

iv   *New South Wales, New Zealand, New Hebrides and the Islands Adjacent*, 1808. Robert Wilkinson (d. ca. 1825). National Library of Australia: nla.map-T1363.

1   *A View of Sydney from Seven Miles*, J.W. Lewin, 1809. State Library of New South Wales: PXA 388 V.3 f.1.

2   *Map of Whittington*. www.old-maps.co.uk © website and database right "Crown Copyright and Landmark Information Group Ltd" (*All rights reserved 2009*).

3   'Evans House' by Henry Bracken, ca. 1930. Watercolour. Presented to the school by John Iliff. Reproduced with the kind permission of Sedbergh School Archive and Heritage Centre.

3   *Portrait of John Dawson (1734–1820)*, 1809. William Whiston Barney, after Joseph Allen. © National Portrait Gallery, London. National Portrait Gallery – UK: D8262.

4   *St Mary the Virgin, Richmond, Marriage Register*. North York County Record Office: PR/RM 1/6.

This page of the register is also in shadow on pp. iii and 9.

5   S.R. Chapman, map relating to the sale of ordnance land near the citadel, Hull, 5/8/1806; Engineer Papers – Northern District, 1797–1811 (National Archives – UK: WO 55/714).

5   *Thomas Dykes (1761–1847) Memorial. Charterhouse, Hull.* Courtesy: The Master, L.S. Deas. Photo: Martin & Lynne Broom.

6   *Revd. Richard Johnson, B.A., Chaplain to the Settlement in New South Wales* (London: Published as the Act directs by Goff & Co., Feby 8, 1787). G. Terry pinxt & sculpt. National Library of Australia: nla.pic-an9594799.

6   *Revd S. Marsden formerly Senior Chaplain of N.S. Wales, and founder of the New Zealand Mission*. Unknown artist. Richard Jones' album. Pencil portrait. State Library of New South Wales: PXA 972/5.

7   Samuel Marsden to Miles Atkinson, 19 May 1803. National Library of Australia: MS 4049.

8   *Station of the Church Missionary Society at Te Puna, Bay of Islands, seen from the SSE, 1840–1849*. Augustus Earle (1793–1838). Oil on wood panel. National Library of Australia: nla.pic-an2260373.

8   Hull Packet, 14 June 1808.

9   Samuel Stones to William Cowper, 17 Jan 1809. Keith Cowper Family Archive.

9   Marriage Licence Allegation, William Cowper & Ann Barrell, 21 Jan 1809. Lambeth Palace Library: FM I/147.

The version of Cowper's signature, which appears on the front cover of the present volume, is also taken from this document.

10 *Port Jackson, New South Wales*, 1825. Augustus Earle (1793–1838). National Library of Australia: nla.pic-an2818282.

11 Title page from William Cowper's copy of John Downame, *Christian Warfare*, 1612 edition. Courtesy & Photo: Tim Cowper. This book has now been deposited in the Mitchell Library, where it joins part 2, *The Contempt of the World* (1619), to complete the library's set.

11 *Stamp, copied, Australia [four pence] Isaac Nichols [first post master] boarding ship in Sydney, 1809*, 1959. National Archives of Australia: C4078, N12078.

12 *Major Johnson announcing the arrest of Governor Bligh*, 1928. Raymond Lindsay. Oil on canvas. Geelong Gallery. Gift of Dame Nellie Melba, 1928. © Estate of the artist.

12 *Requisition to Major Johnson to assume control of the colony*, 26 Jan 1808. State Library of New South Wales: ML Safe 4/5.

Signatures from this document are also in shadow in the present volume on pp.11,14,15,17,18.

13 *St Philip's Church of England Schools plaque, St Philip's Sydney*. Courtesy: St Philip's. Photo: Peter Bolt.

13 *View of part of the river of Sydney, in New South Wales. Taken from St Phillip's church yard*, 1813. Unknown artist. Engraving, printed in black ink, from one copper plate. National Gallery of Australia, Canberra. Purchased 2004.

14 *Henry Cowper examining a Patient under the supervision of William Redfern*, one of the series of postcards, 'Milestones in Medicine', by Parke-Davis (now Pfizer). Used by Permission.

15 *(Old) St Philip's Church*. J. Lewin. State Library of New South Wales: PXD 388 V.1 f.7.

15 *Lachlan Macquarie*, 1822. Richard Read snr. (ca. 1765–1827?). State Library of New South Wales: P2/144.

16 Title page, *The First Report of the Auxiliary Bible Society of NSW* (1817): Courtesy: NSW Bible Society. Photo: John Cowper.

16 *View of the Female Orphan School near Parramatta, New South Wales*, 1825. Joseph Lycett (ca. 1775–1828). Acquatint, hand col. National Library of Australia: nla.pic-an7690892.

17 *Elizabeth Macquarie, Miniature*. Watercolour on ivory miniature in rectangular black wooden frame with oval shaped glass and painted gold edge in centre, and backed in black "American" paper. State Library of New South Wales: MIN 70.

17 *Supreme Court, Sydney*, 1848. Print, engraving. Joseph Fowles (1810–1878). From *Sydney in 1848* (Sydney: J. Fowles, 1849).

18 *A view of the west side of Sydney cove*, [c.1803]. Attributed to George William Evans. State Library of New South Wales: DG V1/73.

19 *Toll Gate and Benevolent Asylum, George Street South*, [1836]. Robert Russell (1808–1900). Lithograph. State Library of New South Wales: Original: PXA 581/7.

20 *North View of Sydney New South Wales*, 1822. Joseph Lycett (ca. 1775–1828). Colour lithograph. State Library of New South Wales: DG v1/11.

21 *Map of the Cowpastures*, Enclosure to J. Macarthur's Additional Memorandum re Land in the Cowpastures, 29 Jan 1823. Mitchell Library: Macarthur Papers, Vol. 66, A2962, 119.

22 Henry Cowper to William Cowper, 16 Sept 1822. Keith Cowper Family Archive.

22 *Female School of Industry*, 1832. William Wilson, engraver (England 1793/1797– Australia 1867). Engraving, printed in black ink, from one plate. National Gallery of Australia, Canberra. Purchased 2004.

23 *The Bethel Flag*. From http://www.sydneybethelunion.com.au.

24 *Native of New south Wales from Wellington Valley*, 1826. Augustus Earle (1793–1838). Watercolour. National Library of Australia: nla.pic-an2818346.

24 *Footstone from grave of Thomas Hobbes Scott*. St John's Whitfield. Photo: Peter Bolt.

25 *Australian Subscription Library*, 1848. Print, engraving. Joseph Fowles (1810–1878). From *Sydney in 1848* (Sydney: J. Fowles, 1849).

25 *Hyde Park, St James Parsonage Dispensary, afterwards the Mint, and Emigration Barracks*, 1842. John Rae. State Library of New South Wales: DG SV*/SpColl/Rae/16.

26 *Major Mitchell sketching the entrance of the caves in Wellington Valley, New South Wales, 1843*. William Romaine Govett (1807–1848). Drawing. National Library of Australia: nla.pic-an4700786.

26 *Ann Cowper (nee Barrell) memorial, St Philip's Sydney*. Courtesy: St Philip's. Photo: Peter Bolt.

27 *Portrait of Harriette Swaine*, [before 1833]. Keith Cowper Family Archive.

27 *Portrait of the Late Right Rev. W. Broughton, Bishop of Sydney, &c*, (Sydney: J.R. Clarke, 1857). Walter G. Mason. Print, wood engraving. National Library of Australia: nla.pic-an7978975.

28 *Rev'd Dr William Cowper, senior chaplain of New South Wales*. Unknown artist. Richard Jones' album. Pencil Portrait, after Read. State Library of New South Wales: PXA 972/4.

29 *Portrait of William Cowper*, 1833. R. Read. Watercolour on cardboard. State Library of New South Wales: P2/236.

31 *Sydney Gazette* 7 Sept 1839. Accessed through the National Library Historic Newspapers. www.nla.gov.au.

32 *Sydney Cove*, ca 1830. Mrs Heriot Anley. State Library of New South Wales: ML 374.

33 *View from Darlinghurst*, 1835. Frederick Garling. Watercolour. State Library of New South Wales: DL Pd 257.

34 *St Philip's Church, Church Hill, St Patrick's Church*, Fleury del., 1853. (Sydney: Sands & Kenny, 1855). Print, engraving. National Library of Australia: nla.pic-an8434132.

34 *Seal attached to William Cowper's Doctor of Divinity Testamur*. Sydney Diocesan Archives: Cowper, William – Personal Papers – Lambeth Doctor of Divinity (1994/75/2). Courtesy: Sydney Diocesan Archives. Photo: Peter Bolt.

35 *Seat of the Revd W. Cowper D.D.* Unknown artist. Richard Jones' album. Watercolour. State Library of New South Wales: PXA 972/19.

36 *Stroud Church*, ca 1854. Conrad Martens (1801–1878). Watercolour and pencil. State Library of New South Wales: V*/Sp Coll/Martens/39.

37 *Letters of Collation of William Cowper*, 24 January 1848. Sydney Diocesan Archives: COWPER William – Personal Papers – 1848 Appointment as Archdeacon of Cumberland (1994/75/1). Courtesy: Sydney Diocesan Archives. Photo: Peter Bolt.

37 *An ecclesiastical relic, Dean Cowper*, 20 Oct 1888. Phil May (1864–1903). Drawing, pen and ink. State Library of New South Wales: SV/134.

38 *(Old) St Philip's Church*, Richard Jones' album. Unknown Artist. State Library of New South Wales: PXA 972/12.

39 *Portrait of the Venerable Archdeacon Cowper, D.D.*, 1854 (Sydney: J.R. Clarke, 1857). Walter G. Mason, after Claxton. Print, wood engraving. National Library of Australia: nla.pic-an7978970.

40 *St Phillips Church*, 1848. Print, engraving. Joseph Fowles (1810–1878). From *Sydney in 1848* (Sydney: J. Fowles, 1849).

40	*Charles Cowper, Premier*. J. Roarty. State Library of New South Wales: PXA 549/24c.
41	*Portrait of Thomas Cowper*, ca. 1850–51. Unknown artist. Watercolour. Warren Kenny Family Archive.
41	*Turning of the turf of the first Australian Railway, Sydney, 3 July 1850*, 1893. John Rae (1813–1900). National Library of Australia: nla.pic-an10759912-S27.
42	*The Government escort and mail containing the gold, arrival at the treasury, Sydney*, 1851. Marshall Claxton (1811–1881). National Library of Australia: nla.pic-an6629355-1.
43	*Appointment of W. Cowper as Bishop Broughton's sole Commissary*. Sydney Diocesan Archives: Bishop of Sydney, Correspondence 1852 (1994/13/10): Courtesy: Sydney Diocesan Archives. Photo: Peter Bolt.
44	*The Hon. Charles Cowper, delegate from New South Wales, 1863*. Wood engraving. State Library of Victoria: IMP04/04/63/8 (b48668).
44	*Portrait of William Macquarie Cowper, Dean of Sydney* (188–?). John Hubert Newman, 1830–1916. National Library of Australia: PIC PIC/7655 LOC Box PIC/7655. nla.pic-an24084521.
45	*Portrait of William Macquarie Cowper*. Australian Town & Country Journal, 22 January 1876, p.133. State Library of New South Wales: TN83.
45	*St Phillip's (now taken down), Church Hill, N.S.W.*, 1852. T.T. Drawing, pencil. National Library of Australia: nla.pic-an5370122.
46	*St Paul's College, Sydney*, 1856. Samuel Thomas Gill (1818–1880). National Library of Australia: nla.pic-an7537510.
47	*Portrait of the Venerable Archdeacon Cowper, D.D.*, Walter G. Mason. *The Illustrated Sydney News*, 28 Jan 1854. Photo: Peter Bolt.
48	*The dining room at Wivenhoe*. Photo: Corinne Cowper.
48	*Elizabeth Ann Cowper*. Keith Cowper Family Archive.
49	*Portrait of Harriette Swaine*, [after 1860]. Photo: E. Steele, Wisbech. Keith Cowper Family Archive.
49	*Moore College, Liverpool, and Thomas Moore's House*, [ca. 1865]. Courtesy: Moore College.
50	*St Philip's Church, Sydney, 1850–1859*. Walter G. Mason. National Library of Australia: nla.pic-an832965.
50	William Cowper to John Cowper, 29 Dec 1856. Stuart Calder Family Archive.
51	*Making the new sewer in Pitt Street, Sydney*. (Sydney: J.R. Clarke, 1857). Walter G. Mason. Print, wood engraving. National Library of Australia: nla.pic-an8021132.
52	*Order of Procession for the funeral of William Cowper*, 9 July 1858. Keith Cowper Family Archive.
52	*Sedgwick Spelman Cowper*. Keith Cowper Family Archive.
52	*Residence of Archdeacon Cowper*, 1860. Frederick Charles Terry, 1826–1869. Drawing, wash. National Library of Australia: nla.pic-an5370153.
53	*Portrait of the Ven. William Cowper, D.D.*, 1854. Marshall Claxton (1811–1881). Courtesy: Warden & Fellows, St Paul's College University of Sydney. Photo: Alice Bolt.
54	*St Philip's, Sydney*, 2009. Photo: Peter Bolt.
Rear Cover	Detail, *Portrait of the Ven. William Cowper, D.D.* 1854. Marshall Claxton (1811–1881). Courtesy: Warden & Fellows, St Paul's College University of Sydney. Photo: Alice Bolt.

Bibliography

FULL NOTES AND REFERENCES CAN BE FOUND IN THE FULL-TEXT biography to which this pictorial edition is a companion. The published works specifically cited or alluded to in the present edition are:

Barker, F. — *The Victor's Crown. A Sermon on the Death of the Venerable W. Cowper, July 12, 1858* (Sydney: Reading & Wellbank, 1858).

Cowper Family, — 'Commemoration of the 175th Anniversary of the arrival at Sydney Cove on 18th August 1809 of the Reverend William Cowper', *CEHSJ* 30.1 (1985), 19–23.

Cowper, W. — *Some Account of Margaret Gold, who died in the Female School of Industry, at Sydney, New South Wales, March 13, 1832, aged Ten Years* (Sydney: Stephens & Stokes, ^{2}1833 [Original: 1832]).

Cowper, W. — *A Brief Memoir of Mrs Susanna Day, who was born December, 1798, and who died 24th April, 1832, at Sydney, in New South Wales* (Sydney: Stephens & Stokes, 21833 [Original: 1832]).

Cowper, W. — *A Sermon [on Psalm 141:7] Preached in St. Philip's Church, Sydney on Sunday, October 14, 1849* (Sydney: W.R. Piddington, [1849]).

Cowper, W. — *The Benefits of Attending Public Worship. A Sermon Delivered in St Philip's New Church on the First Sunday after its Consecration, 30th March, 1856* (Sydney: Reading & Wellbank, 1856).

Cowper, W. — *Thoughts on the Resurrection of the Dead, with Reference to the Millennium* (Sydney: Reading & Wellbank, 1856).

Cowper, W. — *Thoughts on the New Creation, with Reference to the Millennium* (Sydney: Reading & Wellbank, 1856).

Cowper, W. — *Thoughts on the Ages to Come, with Reference to the Millennium* (Sydney: Reading & Wellbank, 1857).

Cowper, W. & Sir Alfred Stephen, — *Correspondence Between Sir Alfred Stephen C.J. and the Ven. Archdeacon Cowper Respecting the Refusal of a License to the Rev. John Milner, B.A.* (Sydney: Reading & Wellbank, 1854).

Cowper, W.M. — *The Autobiography and Reminiscences of William Macquarie Cowper, Dean of Sydney* (Sydney: Angus & Robertson, 1902).

Pridden, W. — *Australia, its History and Present Condition; containing an account both of the bush and of the colonies, with their respective inhabitants* (London: James Burns, 1843).

Wannan, B. — *Early Colonial Scandals. The Turbulent Times of Samuel Marsden* (Melbourne: Landsdowne, 1972 [Original: 1962]).

Personal Acknowledgements

I would like to thank the Cowper200 committee for their invitation to produce this volume, which has been a most enjoyable project. In particular, the support and encouragement given by Jill Auld, John Cowper, and Charles Cowper was wonderfully warm. It was delightful that the biography shook out some exciting material from family archives, and the picture we now have of William has been enriched as a result. Thank you to Keith Cowper, Michael Pain, Stuart Calder, Rod Hirst, Tim Cowper, and Warren Kenny, for their willingness to share the 'family treasures' that have been hidden in their various attics. I am also immensely grateful to Warren Kenny, in particular—the family genealogist who has painstakingly researched the Cowper family for thirty years, and has generously shared his knowledge and information with this newcomer from outside the family. Warren has been quick to answer my questions, always generous with his answers, and patient with my various speculations and half-baked theories. I am also grateful that Warren and Geoff Treloar were willing to read over the manuscript prior to publication, for it is certainly better for their attention. Joy Lankshear has also performed miracles, making the volume a pleasure to the eye.

Even though the subject of this biography won't be reading it—unless the biblical text can be reversed to say, 'though he is dead, he still hears'? (apologies to Hebrews 11:4)—I am grateful for the life of William Cowper and for this opportunity to get to know him just a little, since my own life has been enriched by the experience. Perhaps the biblical text needs to be preserved after all: 'though he is dead, he still speaks'. It has been a privilege to be given this opportunity to listen.

www.ingramcontent.com/pod-product-compliance
Lightning Source LLC
Chambersburg PA
CBHW080902010526
44118CB00016B/2242